ADVANCE PRAISE FOR *IN HER VOICE*:

Women and Hollywood founder and feminist Melissa Silverstein has staked out her territory, and enriched the field, first with her blog and now with this smart, savvy collection of interviews with women directors . . . In Her Voice brings together first-hand accounts of what it's like to be on the front lines of women's filmmaking—and behind the camera, too.

—THELMA ADAMS, Contributing Editor, *Yahoo! Movies*

Melissa Silverstein's media-savvy collection of interviews is an eye-opener. So many talented and accomplished women can only pave the way for more. For me, the revelation is the extraordinary range of interests among these directors, and their incredible ingenuity in getting their projects to the screen. This enterprise fills a huge gap and, unlike a hard-copy book, which starts and stops, In Her Voice *will be an ongoing record of information and celebration.*

—MOLLY HASKELL, film critic and author, *From Reverence to Rape: The Treatment of Women in the Movies* (1974; revised and reissued in 1987) and *Frankly, My Dear: "Gone with the Wind" Revisited*

The contributions of women directors in Hollywood is one of the most over-looked and under-appreciated aspects of the film industry. Melissa Silverstein has compiled a fascinating and illuminating array of interviews of some of the most exciting voices of our time. Kudos :)

—ANGELA ROBINSON, director, D.E.B.S., *Herbie Fully Loaded*

I have followed Melissa's blog ever since she drove a petition to express outrage at the lack female driven films selected for the Cannes film festival this year. The tide is turning but every female director who gets to play ball in Hollywood from now on will owe a debt of gratitude to Melissa's passionate activism on our behalf.

—RACHEL WARD, director, *Beautiful Kate*

Smart and uplifting, this book is a siren call to women to get behind the camera.

—KATE MUIR, Chief Film Critic of *The Times* UK

Melissa has created an incredibly inspiring piece for any filmmaker—not only women. That said, Melissa's book is a great source to learn from other women's experiences and perseverance—for the young or well seasoned!

—BRENDA CHAPMAN, co-director, *Brave*

As a director who began making films in an era without any female role models in Hollywood, I wish I could have had this inspiring collection of interviews by women directors. Their collective experience and advice about the process sends an empowering and passionate message to any woman who wants to enter the business. Just go do it!

—CHRIS HEGEDUS, co-director, *The War Room*

When I first started out making films back in the early 1980s you could count the number or women directing movies on one hand. It's encouraging that three decades later Melissa Silverstein has been able to compile an entire book of interviews with female filmmakers. It's about time someone chronicled this important but overlooked piece of cinema history. However, this is only Volume 1. Let's hope there will soon be Volumes 2 through 10.

—SUSAN SEIDELMAN, director, *Desperately Seeking Susan, The Boynton Beach Club*

There is strength in numbers and strength in these stories. Women directors need never feel alone again.

—CARI BEAUCHAMP, author of *Without Lying Down, Frances Marion and the Powerful Women of Early Hollywood*

In Her Voice *is inspiring in the best, unsentimental sense—smart conversations with working directors who have forged ahead, defying obstacles, to create films that range from the visionary to the crowd-pleasing, and are sometimes both.*

—CARYN JAMES, critic, *Indiewire*

IN HER VOICE

WOMEN DIRECTORS TALK DIRECTING

VOLUME ONE

MELISSA SILVERSTEIN
OF WOMEN AND HOLLYWOOD

with Elizabeth Harper, Heather McLendon, Eva Krainitzki, Laura Shields, Emilie Spiegel

Ordering Information
To order additional copies go to: inhervoice.net
or blogs.indiewire.com/womenandhollywood
Quantity discounts available.

Book design: Shannon Bodie, Lightbourne, Inc.
Front cover photo: ContentWorks.tv, www.istockphoto.com
Author photo: Tina Umlauf

ISBN 978-0-9885764-0-7

CONTENTS

DOCUMENTARIES

PREFACE

All people have a click moment, an experience that deeply affects them and becomes embedded on their psyche. I've heard many women talk about the moment they discovered they were a feminist. Not surprisingly, my click moment has to do with movies and feminism. When I was a teenager I discovered Barbra Streisand, first as a singer and then as an actress. I was sixteen when *Yentl* came out, and I begged my parents—who had no interest in seeing this film—to take me. I remember they drove me on a very cold night to the Syosset Theatre on Long Island to see this film that I was so excited about. (Thanks Mom and Dad.) I was the youngest in the theater by several decades, but I didn't care. I was transfixed throughout the entire movie.

The movie ended and people started to get up, but I stayed glued to my seat. As the credits rolled, I saw something that I had never seen before. A woman's name everywhere. I probably had never thought about it, but seeing it had a profound effect on me. This woman was the producer, the director, the co-writer, the star and the singer. Whatever you might think about the film, you can't help but be impressed with the feat she accomplished. Getting this film made and directing it was not easy. After fifteen years of struggle, she finally got a green light at $14.5 million with the caveat that if it went over budget, Streisand would have to forgo part of her $3 million acting salary to cover the gap (it did go barely over budget to $16.2 million and she had to give back $1.5 million). ["Barbra Puts Her Career on the Line With 'Yentl'—and Learns New Lessons About Her Power and Her Femininity" by Anne Fadiman.]

Looking back to 1983, Streisand's *Yentl* was among other strong women's roles in film that year. It was the year of *Silkwood* and *Terms of Endearment* not to mention *Flashdance*, *Educating Rita*, and *Heart Like a Wheel*. Each of those movies is a classic. *Terms of Endearment* grossed more than $100 million—a sum almost unheard of in the 1980s. But the one thing to remember is that none of those movies, except *Yentl*, was directed by a woman. It was a time of very, very few women directors. It would be wonderful to say that we have progressed to a place thirty years later where what Streisand accomplished has become the norm.

It is true that now there are women working at all levels of the industry. But let's be real, while it is tough for all directors, it is tougher for women. The horrific statistics confirm the anecdotal evidence. Only 5 percent of the top 250 grossing films released in the United States in 2011 were directed by women. And no matter the perception that women have achieved a certain level of success, the numbers are actually getting worse, not better. Women directed 9 percent of films in 1998. Seven percent in 2006, and 7 percent in 2010. (For these statistics and many more, check out the Center for Study of Women in Television and Film at San Diego State University.) Women directors clearly do better in independent film. The latest statistics (from 2011–12) show that women made up 18 percent of narrative film directors and 39 percent of documentary directors of films screened at a large set of film festivals across the United States.

Studio films are still those that get seen by most people and are also the ones that get the largest distribution overseas. The lack of women directors can be partially attributed to the continued rise of the blockbuster, which are most all about male superheroes or male action heroes. When 95 percent of the movies are directed by men, that means we see most movies from a male perspective. I refuse to get into the argument about whether male directors are better than women directors. That is an argument that is so flawed, narrow and sexist that I am not going to dignify it with a response. What I am going to say is that men and women direct differently. Not better, not worse, just different. We have different life experiences and those experiences affect our work.

I also refuse to get into the argument that women's films are not successful. It's true that films directed by men have bigger budgets—which means they have bigger marketing budgets, which means they open on more screens, which means they gross more. Statistics show that it's the budget that affects the gross, not the gender of the director, producer or leading character.

I can count on one hand the women who have directed a film with a budget of more than $100 million—Jennifer Yuh Nelson and Brenda Chapman. They both directed animated films that have been hugely successful. *Kung Fu Panda 2,* directed by Yuh Nelson, grossed more than half a billion just overseas, and *Brave*, co-directed by Chapman, is more than that number for its worldwide gross. And while it has become a regular occurrence to see a male director hit $100 million, because women don't get the big budgeted films, there are relatively few female directors who have achieved that status.

But there are some. Penny Marshall in 1988 was the first woman to direct a movie that grossed $100 million with *Big*. Her film *A League of Their Own* also topped $100 million. Other women who have directed films that have grossed $100 million include, in addition to Yuh Nelson and Chapman: Mimi Leder (*Deep Impact*); Phyllida Lloyd (*Mamma Mia*); Amy Heckerling (*Look Who's Talking*); Catherine Hardwicke (*Twilight*); Anne Fletcher (*The Proposal*); Nora Ephron (*Sleepless in Seattle* and *You've Got Mail*); Penelope Spheeris (*Wayne's World*); Vicky Jenson (*Shrek* and *Shark Tale*); Betty Thomas (*Dr. Doolittle* and *Alvin and the Chipmunks, The Squeakquel*); Nancy Meyers (*What Women Want* and *Something's Gotta Give*).[1]

Another piece of the problem for women directors is the lack of confidence in women's stories. There's a prevailing sense that male stories are universal—for everyone—and that women's stories are just for women. As I wrote in the *New York Times* in a debate on how to get more women into influential positions in Hollywood, I continue to wonder how "the stories of male action heroes became the dominant narratives of our time" when women buy half the movie tickets and are more than half the

---

1. Both Vicky Jenson and Brenda Chapman co-directed their films with men.

population. The reality that women directors and producers and writers deal with is the ongoing perception that women will go see movies about men and that men won't go see stories about women. The success of *Bridesmaids* in 2011 helped diminish the case, because it seemed that for the first time Hollywood noticed men went to see a movie about women. In 2012, other films with women heroes have found success, most notably *The Hunger Games*. But this perception persists as a problem for women directors, especially for those who want to tell women's stories.

Another stumbling block exists for women directors because there are so few women operating at the top tier; so their failures get amplified across the business. We know that there will be directors of both sexes who have films that flop. That's just the way the world works. I look forward to the day when women can make mediocre films and some flops and people just shrug their shoulders and move on.

Even with so many obstructions, women keep fighting to tell their stories and our stories, and I am grateful. That is why I dedicate so much of my work to amplifying their voices. Early on in the work of Women and Hollywood, I decided to get as many female directors to speak with me as possible. So much of the Hollywood conversation is taken up with larger-than-life male personalities that at the end of the day there is not much space for women's voices. The point is: women's voices and their visions matter just as much as men's. Yet, because there are fewer women directing and because their movies don't get as much exposure, we don't hear from them.

My goal with this volume of interviews is to normalize women's voices as directors. Many times when people go to a movie, they don't know or care who directed the film. It's about getting women into the conversations at all levels so that when people start talking about Oscars and other awards each year, there is no surprise when there are multiple women in the mix. Success breeds success. The more women directors who are seen as being able to successfully open a film, the more women directors will get jobs.

This volume presents a wide diversity of directors from features and documentaries—women whose movies were incredibly successful and others who did not achieve commercial success. Some of these films you might not have heard of and others you will be very familiar with. Some directors here have released other movies since our interviews, and others have not yet or may never direct another film.

When I started Women and Hollywood five years ago, I can say with 100 percent truthfulness that I had no idea what I was getting into. Creating the site came from a confluence of activities—doing research for a daily online feminist news update at the Women's Media Center and discovering these things called blogs. As I continued my exploration, it became clear that for the most part none of these blogs talked about women and Hollywood except when they were focused on gossip and fashion, and there were none that covered Hollywood from a feminist angle. I was also becoming increasingly dissatisfied with the movies that I was seeing and realizing how women—especially those over thirty—were completely missing from mainstream Hollywood movies.

People ask me a lot about how the site became a reality, and the truth is one day I woke up and just did it. Came up with the name and started writing. I look at the past work of the blog in three stages. Stage 1 was when it lived on the free platform Blogger. The site consisted mostly of links to stories and updates. Looking back now, Stage 1 was my training ground. It took a while for me and for the site to find a voice. When it (and I) did, after about a year and a half, I moved to a self-hosted site and the new, Stage 2, Women and Hollywood, was born.

An audience was clearly out there for this information and the site continued to grow. In Stage 3 of the site, it got picked up and moved to Indiewire in early 2011. Being on Indiewire gives the site a level of professionalism and acceptance that is unachievable as an individual blogger.

Now as we hit the fifth anniversary of the site, I see it entering Stage 4. It's about making change, and it's about amplifying other women's voices and visions. I spent a decade working under some of the most effective feminist changemakers of our time. Their work and their passion are in my bones. I never got into this to hear my own voice. This was always about bringing women's voices into the conversation. And that is one reason why the blog is so focused on interviews. To bring the voices of women working at all levels of the business into the conversation.

Some information about this book:

- All the interviews contained here first appeared on the site Women and Hollywood.
- Some have been edited for clarity.
- This volume includes interviews from the first three years of the site. We hope to have another volume in the near future that will cover later years.
- Because of the difficulty in getting legal clearances to republish material, not all the Women and Hollywood director interviews are included here, and not all the interviews are accompanied by photographs.
- Each entry contains links to trailers and to the IMDb site for the film. We also include a short biography of the director.
- There are also descriptions and some reviews of the films, mostly from Women and Hollywood. Information from elsewhere is credited to the appropriate site.

FEATURES

Wendy Jo Carlton

FILM TITLE: *Hannah Free*

Date of Release (or festival premiere): 2009 Frameline LGBT Film Festival

Link to IMDb Page: www.imdb.com/title/tt1315214

Link to Film Site: www.hannahfree.com

Link to Trailer: www.hannahfree.com/hannah_free_trailer1.html

BIO: Wendy Jo Carlton is a filmmaker, writer, and photographer with a background in radio production, teaching, and media activism. Carlton is a former artist-in-residence at 911 Media Arts in Seattle and a recipient of the Navona Fellowship from the University of Illinois Chicago, where she earned a graduate degree in film/new media. Her award-winning narrative and experimental short films have screened internationally, including at the American Film Institute, Sundance, and many other festivals.

In addition to founding a media literacy program for teen girls called Chicks Make Flicks, Carlton works as a field producer for Sirius Radio and PBS Television and teaches at Columbia College. She recently finished her third feature film, "Jamie and Jessie Are Not Together," which she wrote and directed. (Credit: Wendy Jo Carlton Website)

DESCRIPTION: *Hannah Free* tells the story of a life-long love affair between two women, Hannah and Rachel. Hannah (Sharon Gless) is a free spirit who refuses to abide by the rules and has constant wanderlust even though she deeply loves Rachel. It takes Rachel a lot longer to fully be with Hannah even though she does love her. Their struggle to love each other and be accepted is symbolic of the evolution of the struggle for gay civil rights.

Gless is a forceful presence as Hannah. While the story might seem cutting edge because it is about two women, it really isn't—it's a plain old love story that just happens to be about two women. I love that we see the women age through the film, which moves it beyond the "cool" factor. This is a story that is happening in communities all across the country, and I like that it was brought out from behind the shadows into the forefront.

Interview Date: June 25, 2009

WOMEN AND HOLLYWOOD: **How did you become involved with this film?**

WENDY JO CARLTON: I've been an independent filmmaker for about twenty years, and had many successful shorts and a few screenplays under my belt before I moved from Seattle to Chicago. I worked with Tracy Baim, the executive producer, on a couple other projects, the Chicago Gay Games DVD and recently the living library that is the Chicago Gay History Project. In the course of interviewing hundreds of LGBT folks in the area, I met the playwright Claudia Allen and then the three of us decided to make a lesbian feature film in Chicago, adapting *Hannah Free*, one of Claudia's popular plays.

W&H: **There are not many films that show lesbians in this way. Do you think this is a breakthrough in how lesbians will be seen on film?**

WJC: It was important to me to portray Hannah and Rachel not just as young lovers but as older lovers as well, two women who share a deep emotional connection but also a passionate physical and sexual connection. And I didn't want to just imply that, but wanted to show their attraction visually and cinematically. Most mainstream feature films don't show older couples sharing physical affection and sexual attraction for one another. Whether they are straight or queer, we just don't see many older characters in bed together or see older people kissing and being sensual together onscreen. I think it's sexy, fun, and life affirming.

Most long-term romantic relationships, regardless of orientation, wax and wane in the lust department. What's great about Hannah and Rachel is that theirs is the kind of great love affair that has sustained its passion over decades—the kind of fantastic, enduring attraction and love that is celebrated and pined for in straight films all the time.

W&H: **How did Sharon Gless get involved?**

WJC: Sharon Gless and Claudia Allen are old pals because Sharon came to Chicago years ago to star in one of Claudia's plays called *Cahoots*. They maintained a friendship and when Claudia sent Sharon the script, she decided to come back to Chicago and take on the complex and demanding role of Hannah. She did an incredible job and brings so much complexity, nuance, humor, and gravitas to the role.

W&H: **How can this film break out from the gay and lesbian film circuit into the mainstream?**

WJC: I think this film is very entertaining, sensual, and provocative as a story of a great love affair. It's universal and will engage viewers regardless of sexual orientation. Hannah is a dynamic, sexy, flawed, passionate human being, and who can't relate to that? And Sharon Gless is such a pleasure to watch in every scene.

W&H: **How long did it take to get the film made?**

WJC: The film has taken a little less than a year from start to finish— I don't know how we managed it!

W&H: **What advice do you have for women filmmakers?**

WJC: Find some mentors because when things aren't going well, a good mentor—male or female—is someone who believes in you and can help keep you focused and encouraged, and help you make the right connections.

Also, I think it's been said before, but it bears repeating, explore your personal obsessions. It helps make for more original storytelling. And give yourself permission to be funny, idiosyncratic, and raunchy.

W&H: **Because of all the Proposition 8 craziness, do you plan on using the attention the gay marriage issue is getting to get the word out on your film?**

WJC: I think the film really helps put a human face on the issue. Prop 8 is insane and unjust. It makes me very sad that we still live in a culture where people are allowed to vote on who should remain second-class citizens. If we had allowed majority votes on civil and basic human rights, women and blacks still wouldn't have the right to vote.

W&H: **When people walk out of the theater after seeing your film, what do you want them to be thinking about?**

WJC: My favorite subject—the power and mystery of love. Although the movie has its sadder moments, it also has quite a bit of humor, so I hope people are moved and entertained. And, ultimately, it's a triumph of the human spirit. *Hannah Free* represents all the beautiful, brave queer women and men who've insisted on living their truth and on loving both who they are and whoever they want.

Photo Credit: Thierry Van Biesen

Cherien Dabis

FILM TITLE: *Amreeka*

Date of Release (or festival premiere): 2009 Sundance Film Festival

Link to IMDb Page: www.imdb.com/title/tt1190858

Link to Site: www.amreeka.com

Link to Trailer: www.amreeka.com

B I O : Named one of *Variety*'s "Ten Directors to Watch" in 2009, award-winning independent filmmaker Cherien Dabis made her feature writing and directorial debut with *Amreeka*, which premiered to both audience and critical acclaim in the U.S. Dramatic Competition at the 2009 Sundance Film Festival. At Tribeca All Access in 2007, Dabis was honored with the first-ever L'Oréal Paris Women of Worth Vision Award, and last year she won the Renew Media/Tribeca Film Institute's Media Artist Fellowship, funded by the Rockefeller Foundation. Also a television writer and producer, Dabis worked on Showtime Network's groundbreaking, original hit series *The L Word* for three seasons. A graduate of Columbia University's MFA film program, she has written, directed, and produced several short films, which have screened at some of the world's top film festivals. The first of her family born in the United States, Dabis was raised in Ohio and Jordan, and currently resides in New York City.

DESCRIPTION: *Amreeka* tells the story of Muna, a Palestinian, who immigrates to the United States with her teenage son, Fadi, right after the first U.S. invasion of Iraq. Life in America is not the typical "American Dream" for Muna, who has a hard time finding a job and winds up flipping burgers at White Castle. Life is hard for Fadi, too, as he tries to acclimate into a midwestern American high school where the kids think that everyone who is Muslim and from the Middle East is now the enemy. This film gives a real and honest assessment of what it's like to be an "outsider" trying to fit into mainstream culture while also trying to keep your own cultural identity. The performances are heartfelt, especially from Nisreen Faour as Muna. Hiam Abbass co-stars as Muna's sister.

Interview Date: January 21, 2009

WOMEN AND HOLLYWOOD: What made you want to make this film?

CHERIEN DABIS: The story is quite personal, inspired by my family
and loosely based on true events. I grew up in a small town in
Ohio of about ten thousand people. I actually grew up between
Ohio and Jordan but most of my time was spent in this small
town where as Arab Americans, we were isolated because there
was no Arab community and not a whole lot of diversity. For
a while, everything was fine, and we fit in relatively well until
the first Gulf War. Then they scapegoated my family and,
overnight, we virtually became the enemy. All kinds of absurd
things happened. My father, who is a physician, lost many of
his patients because they wouldn't support an Arab doctor;
and then it came to a head when the Secret Service came to my
high school to investigate a rumor that my seventeen-year-old
sister threatened to kill the president.

It was an eye-opening event, my coming of age. I became
politicized, and very aware of the media and how the media
were perpetuating the stereotypes that were directly affecting
us. So I decided to become a storyteller. I don't know if it was
as conscious a decision as that, but I knew that I wanted to do
something to change the way the media related to Arabs, to
change the way we were represented. I also wanted to change
the fact that we are underrepresented. I simply wanted to get
our stories out there—we have so many and I thought if people
could see it from our point of view, they would realize how
funny and absurd it is.

W&H: **Is the film contemporary?**

CD: The film is relatively contemporary. It's a soft period piece and
takes place during the second Iraq invasion in 2003.

W&H: **You are trying to give a different vision of Arabs and break through typical Hollywood stereotypes.**

CD: People can be lazy in their storytelling and then characters become one-dimensional and easy to villanize. Then it becomes the story of good vs. evil rather than people are people. It's easy to fall back on the formulaic stereotypes, and I think it is much more difficult to create characters that are complex, rich, and multidimensional.

W&H: **This film seems quite timely with what just happened in the Middle East.**

CD: The film is not really political. It's political in context, but the heart of the story is the relationship between the mother and son. It's the story of a woman who desperately wants to secure a better future for her son and will do anything for him including leave her homeland and start over completely. She wants to flee her controlling mother, her failed marriage, and start anew to get to be someone else, somewhere else. The backdrop of the film is the adversity they have to overcome, and the stereotypes and prejudices that people have about Arabs. These are some of the challenges she faces, but she is optimistic and hopeful, and she surprises others with her optimism.

W&H: **Do you think it's a good time for this film to come out? Will people be more receptive to it now?**

CD: Absolutely. We have a president with an Arab middle name. He's the first African American president. There is a feeling of hope. It's a new era. Barack Obama represents the new America and in some way my film represents the America that this country should be. What this country could be if people were a little more open, friendly, trusting, and accepting—like Muna. So much of this business is about timing, and the timing is really good with the change in the administration.

W&H: **It's hard for people to make films nowadays, harder for women's stories, harder for a woman writer and director, and even harder for stories about women of color. Talk about the struggles to get this film made.**

CD: I started writing it in 2003 when I was a graduate student at Columbia studying film. I already spoke about my experience in 1991, and exactly a decade later, in September 2001, I moved to New York and started film school. It was surreal to be in New York right after 9/11 and what was happening set the tone for my film school experience; 9/11 got many people to stop and think, "What am I doing with my life and why am I doing what I chose to do?" It made everyone reevaluate where they were, and it was especially true for people in film school because film seemed so frivolous at the time. People were going to donate blood and we were making movies—who cares? That was the feeling for a little while after 9/11.

For me, it reminded me of the reason why I became a film-maker. I was hearing stories of Middle Easterners being scape-goated, once more. And then the United States invaded Iraq again, and history was literally repeating itself. That was when I said, "OK, I have to sit down and write this story." The world is ready for a Palestinian immigrant story, one that can reach mainstream audiences. I was aware of not wanting it to be political, I wanted it to have humor, and I want people to see it. I don't want it to be ghettoized because I didn't make it just for the Arab community.

W&H: **What do you want them to think about when they leave the film?**

CD: I want them to really fall in love with the characters. It's a glimpse into a world they might not see otherwise. I want them to walk away knowing that the culture is beautiful and should be appreciated and that stereotypes are unnecessary. I want them to walk away with a feeling of love and hope that they have just met people they really liked.

W&H: **Talk about the Sundance experience.**

CD: It's been a whirlwind.

W&H: **What was the biggest high?**

CD: My world premiere was on Saturday afternoon at the Eccles Theatre, which seats fourteen hundred people, and it was entirely packed. It was such a thrill and I was so nervous. I had to introduce the film and was sad that my mother couldn't be there so I called her on my cell phone and had her on the phone while I introduced the film and had everyone said "hi" to her. Everyone shouted, "Hi mom." I got so emotional, and she was giggling and sobbing. It was such a sweet moment, one I will never forget. Then the movie started and everyone was laughing in the right places; they were so with the film and afterward, there was a standing ovation. It was a magical moment.

W&H: **The films about guys are generating most of the buzz. Have you noticed that?**

CD: Yes, it's interesting. I have noticed that it is easier to get a film with a male lead financed, and to get those movies seen and sold, and I don't know why. On the other hand, I wasn't prepared for how tremendously positive the response has been for this movie. In some ways, it is the perfect reception and maybe if it was not such a difficult market, we would have sold the film already. But I am hopeful and the prospects seem good.

[Note: *Amreeka* was released by National Geographic Films in September 2009.]

Photo Credit: Columbia University School of the Arts

Katherine Dieckmann

FILM TITLE: *Motherhood*

Date of Release (or festival premiere): March 5, 2010

Link to IMDb Page: www.imdb.com/title/tt1220220

Link to Trailer: www.youtube.com/watch?v=SeHtiGSh4aE

BIO: Writer-director Katherine Dieckmann began her directing career by directing music videos for such bands as R.E.M., Wilco, Aimee Mann, and Everything But the Girl, and was the originating director on Nickelodeon's groundbreaking live action children's serial, *The Adventures of Pete & Pete*, for which she received a CableAce nomination for Best Direction of a Comedy Special. An assistant professor in the Film Division of Columbia University's Graduate School of the Arts, where she teaches screenwriting, Dieckmann lives in New York City and upstate New York with her husband and two children.

DESCRIPTION: *Motherhood*, starring Uma Thurman, Anthony Edwards, and Minnie Driver, is a day-in-the-life comedy that tracks a harried mother's identity crisis on the day she has to throw her daughter's birthday party. In addition to making plans for the party, Eliza Welch decides to enter a blogging contest for a parenting magazine that asks contestants, "What Does Motherhood Mean to Me?" As one thing after another goes horribly wrong on this fateful day, Eliza finds her answer to that question.

Interview Date: October 30, 2009

WOMEN AND HOLLYWOOD: You said in the *New York Times* recently that a man can write great women's movies but you don't think a man could have written this story. Can you elaborate?

KATHERINE DIECKMANN: Think about a movie like *You Can Count on Me*. I think that in some ways it's a very female movie in the orientation of the writing. But I think that until you have really been inside the experience of being a mother you can't understand the cultural and pragmatic obstacles are. That's what I meant by that.

W&H: So many female directors don't want to be known only as directors of women but with this film you seem to be embracing it.

KD: I am, but I have made two films with men at the center so I really don't think that's true. I made this particular film very much from my perspective as a woman. The film I am writing now has a gay man at the center. The movie I made before this, *Diggers*, has four hetero guys at the center. To me, I don't want to be known as a women's director. However, I still feel that female subject matter is really underserved in film and is vitally important to me even though I like all kinds of movies.

W&H: I feel I must clarify, I didn't mean to imply that as a woman you should only direct movies about women, but there is something about the term. Can you ever see a guy called a male director? It's the labeling.

KD: Yes, it's about diminishing and controlling, and I don't feel like being diminished or controlled in that sense. But I think we still haven't figured out in this culture how to allow the female director to have a kind of iconic power. I was struck a couple of years ago when *Variety* did an issue commemorating Brett Ratner breaking the billion-dollar mark for his movies. All the photographs were of these guys clasping Brett on the arm saying something like "well done, dude." There were no women in those pictures. And I thought what woman director could you cut out and put in Brett Ratner's place shaking hands with Bob Evans passing along the legacy vibe. No, that doesn't exist and that's what I mean by the iconic image of the woman director. I read somewhere that directing is always talked about in terms of war and sports metaphors. I went into battle. I was on the playing field. I don't really think about my work that way. That's a foreign language to me, and I think culturally that is how directing gets talked about.

W&H: **There still seems to be a glass ceiling for women directors.
        Things are not getting better, they are getting worse.**

KD: I think that's true.

W&H: **What do you think about breaking it down?**

KD: We don't think about breaking it down because that's too dis-
        couraging. I think every woman director I know, and I know a
        bunch of them—Mary Harron, Alison Maclean, Nancy Savoca,
        Mira Nair—find that they (not just the women but the men
        too) are enormously supportive of each other's endeavors. Most
        women directors I know are really focused on how am I going
        to get my next movie made. This movie I am trying to make
        called *The Shags* is about an all-girl band, and I was trying
        to get the script to Kirsten Dunst. A friend of mine knew the
        director, Peyton Reed, who directed *Bring It On,* and I got in
        touch with him and he didn't know me but he read the script
        and gave it to Kirsten. So I feel within this circuit of people
        making movies there is an enormous tendency to try and
        support each other from both women and men.

        The system is another issue. When people ask if I have ever
        encountered sexism on shoots, I honestly say I haven't. I've
        worked with lots of guys and I've never found gender to be a
        problem in the pragmatics of doing things. I think gender is a
        problem in the global picture of what gets made, how people
        get hired, and how the profession is perceived.

W&H: **There doesn't seem to be any will for change?**

KD: There is a real tendency to ignore, as has widely been
        remarked, the successes of women-made movies. It's like they
        are pushed under the carpet and you have to fight the battle
        all over again against the perception that they don't do well.
        They do do well. That's why I am curious about *Motherhood*

because we are self-distributing, and I've been doing interviews with mom bloggers and the actresses and we are doing this more grass-roots approach including a breast cancer benefit, where $1 from ticket sales on Fandango will go to breast cancer research. We are trying to move things out through different channels.

W&H: **The term *mommy blogger* is kind of loaded nowadays. Did you know what you were walking into?**

KD: I've noticed. I have to admit when I wrote my script I had never read a mom blog. I had no idea. Originally when I wrote the script, the character was a journalist because that's what I knew, but it didn't work and I thought that mom blogging was interesting because it has to do with this issue of voice and finding an outlet for your voice. Why do you say it's loaded?

W&H: **Because of the way they are treated in the culture.**

KD: I think it's a very complicated issue. I feel it's really important for women to be able to talk about the experiences they have that are so denigrated by the culture, and I think it's really important to be able to move beyond those experiences sometimes to talk about other things. So it is both. There needs to be an outlet for expression about "dailyness" because that is what your life is and that is what sustains the human race, and it is not to be trivialized. However, for myself, I can't imagine anything worse than having to talk about mommy topics all day long. That's not what I want to do.

I feel that *Motherhood* has invisible content, like at the beginning of the film in the credits where Uma's character is scurrying around and making the coffee and feeding the banana to her kid. It's all very whimsical but in fact her husband gets up and toasts himself some bread and sits back down to read and nobody sees that as off. It's what we see all the time. It's the beginning of the cycle of exhaustion, and when people ask me why she is so tired, I say did you miss all the things she just did? That's what I mean about a woman writing the script. You have to know the fatigue and the erosion of self-esteem for which that kind of menial mundanity induces in most people except the weirdly and endlessly self-sacrificing ones.

W&H:　**The producers on this film are women. Did you seek out female producers for this?**

KD:　I met with a lot of men I really like about producing this film, but I felt at the end of the day that I needed to go with Rachel Cohen. She and I have been friends for a decade, and I feel intellectually, politically, and spiritually aligned with her. She took it and found the money, and I trusted her and knew she would have my back. She did and was there for me every step of the way. I felt the same about Pam Koffler from Killer Films whom I had known for a long time socially and whom I had talked to about the script before I had even started to write it. I felt that these women really get me and get why I am doing this, and I will be safe.

W&H:　**You talked a little about the current obsession with the "Aptowian" comedy films today. How did it become such a fixation?**

KD:　I love and hate those movies at the same time. Politically I hate them, but I love watching them. I think there is a great confusion culturally about men's and women's roles and to me Judd Apatow movies really reflect that confusion. Women, for all the difficulties that we face, are increasingly assured in the world. I really do think that. There is such anxiety in men about how they are supposed to be, and so this is a hysterical reaction to it. I think it will be interesting to see how it shakes out in the next few years.

W&H: **What is the message you want people to get after seeing the film?**

KD: The message I am trying to say, and it's not just a motherhood message, is to challenge yourself and also be accepting. This character is doing neither in the beginning of the movie. She is neither challenging herself nor accepting the limitations of what her reality is and that has a lot to do with malcontent, and nobody likes a malcontented person. Many mothers are malcontented because there are real limitations to the ways you can live your life as a mother, economic and practical. So I think on the one hand some things can be changed, but like I said in the *New York Times* piece, I think it's really easy to hide behind motherhood. Women have to challenge themselves not to do that because it's easy. If they want to say something or do something, they can't use motherhood as an excuse to avoid trying to do it.

W&H: **Do you think you will get some backlash from some moms?**

KD: Maybe. I don't think I am saying don't be a stay-at-home mom or don't view mothering as a primary impetus in a certain phase of your life, but let's face it, it is a short phase of your life and as your children get older, they won't need you in that way, and they won't if you've done your job right. So figure out who you are. Who are you at the end of the day? Who are you apart from mom? I feel that's the essential question of the movie. This woman doesn't know who she is apart from mom anymore, and I think many women experience that weirdly dissociative state when they become mothers.

W&H: **What advice do you have for women filmmakers?**

KD: Tenacity and determination. I teach screenwriting at Columbia and I had a wonderful student really succeed with her feature in the last year—Cherien Dabis with *Amreeka*. Cherien had such focus and she rewrote that script—I must have read ten drafts of that script—she worked and worked and worked and was savvy and persistent in the loveliest way and made a really good first film. I think it takes for anyone, but especially women, an unbelievable persistence and really believing in what you have to say.

Alison Eastwood

FILM TITLE: *Rails & Ties*

Date of Release (or festival premiere): 2007 Telluride Film Festival

Link to IMDb Page: www.imdb.com/title/tt0822849/

Link to Trailer: http://youtu.be/nRSNOodc708

BIO: Alison Eastwood began her film career as an actress, performing in such films as *Bronco Billy*, *Tightrope*, *Midnight in the Garden of Good and Evil*, *Breakfast of Champions*, and *Poolhall Junkies*. *Rails & Ties* was her directing debut in 2007, and she currently working on her second film, *Battlecreek,* as both director and producer.

DESCRIPTION: Alison Eastwood makes her directing debut with the small budget ($7m) drama *Rails & Ties*. The film is a powerful story of love and loss, in which Marcia Gay Harden and Kevin Bacon give Oscar®-caliber performances.

Interview Date: October 24, 2007

WOMEN AND HOLLYWOOD: **What was it about this script that made you want to direct the film?**

ALISON EASTWOOD: Originally, I had attached myself as a producer and after a couple of years living with the script and working with the writer [Micky Levy, a woman], I just grew to love these characters. I found them very real and touching and even though Kevin Bacon's character, Tom, is a very shut down person, I know people like that. I liked the ideas, the subject matter. Everyone deals with tragedy and loss but the idea is that through unsavory circumstances, you can still find a way to have connections.

W&H: **This is an intimate, almost theatrical film not usually released by the major studios nowadays. How did you get this made?**

AE: It was initially financed through Warner Independent. The situation with WB distributing came about because Warner Independent is a much smaller division. They had a few films coming out this year, and they really weren't capable of distributing and marketing the film. I really lobbied for it to come out this year. Films that are more character driven and deep usually come out in the fall, and I just didn't want to wait until next year. I'm lucky because a big studio is willing to get behind a small film with great actors.

W&H: **This summer both of Lawrence Kasdan's sons had films come out and I asked myself "Where are the daughters?" [Sofia Coppola is the most prominent and only director daughter I can think of]. As the daughter of a director [Alison's father is Clint Eastwood], what was it like becoming a director?**

AE: It felt natural. Subconsciously, I didn't want to get into directing because I've lived in the shadow and was trying to be an actress. Somewhere I thought I just don't want to go there. But I felt inspired by the story and it felt natural. He [dad, Clint] always made it look easy (though I know it isn't), enjoyable, and collaborative.

W&H: **Why aren't there more women directing films?**

AE: I think the biggest problem is that Hollywood is a boys club and has been for a long time. It's shifting but we need to keep pushing ahead and developing projects and sticking together. I don't want to sound like a feminist, but we have to band together.

W&H: **You don't want to sound like a feminist?**

AE: Well, I don't really like that term. It has always sounded a little radical to me. I certainly believe in equal rights for women, but I also believe there is a way of doing things more subtly. The media makes it a negative term, and I feel things can be done without being in your face or angry but showing by example.

In Hollywood, there are more women producers and actresses commanding bigger roles and bigger salaries and have production deals and production companies. It's just a matter of continuing to move forward and it will take a long time but since the '30s and '40s, we've come a long way.

It's just a matter of doing good work. It doesn't matter if you are a man or woman; if your work is shabby, you're not going to get any respect.

W&H: **Did you bring different things to this script because you are a woman?**

AE: I don't think a man would have picked this script. I found it to be emotional and touching. It meant a lot to me.

Photo Credit: Brian Kavanaugh-Jones

Shana Feste

FILM TITLE: *The Greatest*

Date of Release (or festival premiere): 2009 Sundance Film Festival

Link to IMDb page: www.imdb.com/title/tt1226232

Link to Trailer: http://youtu.be/TfjNuq9Yq3s

BIO: A graduate of the American Film Institute, Shana Feste has been named
one of *Variety*'s "Ten Directors to Watch" and one of *Filmmaker Magazine*'s "25
New Faces in Independent Film." She was nominated for a Humanitas Prize
for her first feature, *The Greatest*, which she both wrote and directed. Starring
Oscar®-nominee Carey Mulligan, Oscar®-winner Susan Sarandon, and Pierce
Brosnan, the film premiered at Sundance in 2009 and was released by Paladin in
2010. *Country Strong*, Shana's second directorial effort that she also wrote, was
released in 2010 by Screen Gems. Starring Oscar®-winner Gwyneth Paltrow,
Tim McGraw, Garrett Hedlund, and Leighton Meester, the film earned both
Golden Globe and Academy Award nominations for Best Original Song.
Shana is currently attached to write and direct an adaptation of
Carolyn Turgeon's novel *Mermaid: A Twist on the Classic Tale*.

DESCRIPTION: *The Greatest* is the story of how a family reconnects after the loss of a child. It is a meditation on grief. Susan Sarandon is a pro at these types of flicks, but I also found Pierce Brosnan's performance very moving. The family indie film—especially one imbued with such sadness—are hard to get done so it is a testament to first time writer and director Shana Feste that we are even seeing this film at all.

Interview Date April 2, 2010

WOMEN AND HOLLYWOOD: **This is your first writing and directing effort. How were you able to secure such a stellar cast?**

SHANA FESTE: The financing would only be triggered if we secured A-list talent, so we were determined to get actors' attention. Pierce [Brosnan] and Susan [Sarandon] were always dreams of ours but totally unrealistic dreams—we were a low-budget film with a first-time director—not really an actor magnet. With the help of CAA, we got the script to Pierce's producing partner, Beau St. Clair, and she convinced Pierce to read the script. Susan read it at about the same time (through her agents at ICM), and they both responded to the roles and wanted to work together. I met with them and pleaded my case very passionately and they said yes. It was pretty amazing and a testament to them as artists because not many actors at their level would take such a big risk on a first-time director.

We got really lucky with Carey [Mulligan]. At the time we were casting she was not well known—she had just finished *An Education*, but we hadn't seen it, we had only spoken with one of the producers who said she was brilliant. We saw a lot of girls for this role—girls with a lot more experience than Carey—but no one could touch her as an actress. She is truly gifted, and we were lucky enough to get her at a time when she would have us!

W&H: **Not many people are drawn to family dramas, especially ones that focus on grief. What made you want to tell this type of story?**

SF: I'm pretty odd in that I am drawn to family dramas, I guess. I love watching them, writing them, making them. I think as a writer you have to prepare yourself for a really solitary experience and the characters you write are going to be your only company so you better like them. I loved writing these characters and, without sounding totally nuts, they became my friends and I wanted to take care of them, to see them through this heartbreaking journey. The most important thing in a family drama is character, so the genre seems like a natural fit for me. I think as a writer you also set out to fix the problems within your own family and this was an opportunity to show a family that stays connected during a very difficult time.

W&H: **Did you always have it in mind that you were going to direct the film? Was that a hard sell to investors?**

SF: I did always know and said that I would like to direct this film.
        That's the advantage to writing your own material—you can
        attach yourself to your script and no one can take it away from
        you. It's why I will always try and write my own material. I also
        prepared a large visual scrapbook inspired by Bruce Block's
        book on visual storytelling, which I showed to the investors
        and producers. It had photographs of all my ideas on tone,
        camera movement, color, space, and lines. It gave them confi-
        dence in me as a filmmaker.

W&H: **Some of the strongest moments in the film are the silent
        ones—how hard was it to keep those moments in?**

SF: It was difficult. There is one shot in the film that lasts for more
        than two minutes and we never cut away from it. I met with
        a bit of resistance to it, for sure, but I was very steadfast in my
        reasons for wanting it in the film. For me, the actor's body
        language alone set up their broken family dynamic—it was also
        some of Pierce's best work. I pushed really hard for that shot
        to stay in the film and it was a risk. As a first-time director, it's
        hard to make passionate cases for things when you really have
        no idea if it will work—you're just going off your gut. I'm just
        thankful my producers supported me and let me keep it in the
        movie. I've been studying directing with Judith Weston, and
        we did a wonderful exercise in her class where we had actors
        perform one of our scenes without using dialogue—it was sur-
        prising to see how much could be accomplished with just looks
        and how tempting it is as a writer to overwrite scenes.

W&H: **How bizarre it must have been to have your film get into
        Sundance the year that your star Carey Mulligan became the
        "it" girl of the festival. Did it help your film?**

SF: I think Carey helped our film tremendously. It was incredibly
        gratifying to watch people fall in love with her at Sundance.

She so deserves it. We went into Sundance with two movie stars and came out with three, which was wonderful.

W&H: **It's been more than a year since the film debuted at Sundance. Talk a bit about how you sold the film and the decision to release it now.**

SF: We were lucky enough to receive multiple offers at Sundance, and we decided to go with Senator because of Mark Urman's incredible passion for the film. Senator went out of business a few months later which was heartbreaking, but luckily, Mark formed a new company, Paladin, and we kept the film with him. The ironic thing is that even at Sundance we wanted to release *The Greatest* in March or April. We felt that the fall was too congested and if we waited until after *An Education* was released, we could capitalize on Carey's incredible performance and budding success.

W&H: **Do you think that Kathryn Bigelow's Oscar win will open up more opportunities for female directors?**

SF: I hope so. I think part of the reason it took me so long to publicly call myself a director was because I didn't have many female directors as role models. When I was in high school, Steven Spielberg, James Cameron, and Spike Lee were the household names. Hopefully, now Kathryn Bigelow will be one and young girls will start calling themselves directors a lot sooner than I did. Because that's half the battle won.

W&H: **What are you doing next?**

SF: I just finished shooting a drama about country music starring Gwyneth Paltrow, Tim McGraw, Leighton Meester, and Garrett Hedlund, in Nashville. It will be released in the fall of this year by Sony Screengems.

W&H: **What advice do you have for female directors?**

SF: I think the smartest thing I did was to work with other women. I've only worked with women producers and it has always been an amazing experience. So my advice to the women reading this would be to work with and support other women!

Photo Credit: Sebastian Mlynarski

Debra Granik

FILM TITLE: *Winter's Bone*

Date of Release (or festival premiere): 2010 Sundance Film Festival

Link to IMDb page: www.imdb.com/title/tt1399683

Link to Site: www.wintersbonemovie.com

Link to Trailer: www.youtube.com/watch?v=bE_X2pDRXyY

BIO: Debra Granik attended the Graduate Film Program at New York University where she won awards for her short film, *Snake Feed*. She attended both the Writers and Directors Lab at the Sundance Institute where she developed *Snake Feed* into a feature film script. Debra premiered her first feature film, *Down to the Bone*, at the Sundance Film Festival in 2004, where she won the Best Director Award. *Down to the Bone* went on to screen at film festivals worldwide and won the International Critics Prize at the Vienna Film Festival, amongst others. In 2009, she directed *Winter's Bone* in the Missouri Ozarks, which was nominated for three Academy Awards.

DESCRIPTION: *Winter's Bone* tells the story of seventeen-year-old Ree Dolly (Jennifer Lawrence), a girl who has to grow up too fast because she has to take care of her whole family, including her mentally ill mother. In addition to this immense responsibility, she has to find her father and make sure he doesn't miss his court date or else she will lose the house. The stakes are so very high, and her desperation is palpable. She treads into territory and confronts dangerous people to get her answers. But her determination and resilience and love for her family will not let her give up.

This is director Debra Granik's second film. Her first, *Down to the Bone*, introduced all of us to Vera Farmiga. Granik is not only a director here; she's an anthropologist, introducing us to a community of people that most people in urban and suburban settings never get to see. We don't see rural America because it is hard to watch. But watch we should because this is a film that should not be missed. It is that good. I can't wait to see it again.

Interview Date: June 11, 2010

WOMEN AND HOLLYWOOD: How were you drawn to the project?

DEBRA GRANIK: I read the book and found a really strong enticing
female heroine—the protagonist who I had been waiting
for. And Anne (Rosellini), who made the film with me and
co-wrote the screenplay, felt something similar. We just had
a really excellent moment where we looked at each other and
said, "Oh, my God, this feels so different from what we have
been reading." I was just so excited—it was a full depiction of
a *person*. She didn't just have to have one strong characteristic.
She could be many things. What is interesting is that, in the
story, the actual parts of her being a teen aren't really shown.
Parts of her normal, civilian life aren't shown. This film is so
condensed in terms of what it can take on. The book had these
parameters where Ree (Jennifer Lawrence) has a very limited
time to solve something. It's very pressing. The stakes are very
high. We were given this gift where we didn't have to engage
with all aspects of her existence. We have to see her perform
this part of her life with a lot of rigor, and she also has this
boldness and moxie, if you will. But she also has this deep
concern for her siblings, the ability to nurture them and to be
immensely protective of them.

W&H: **Without being parented herself.**

DG: Clearly, she has learned some important things. Before her
dad was cut off from them, he had instructed her in a way that
seemed thoroughly about survival. Her mom is dealing with
depression and is really not in good shape. But she does recognize that around her there are very *happening* women. Her
girlfriend Gail (Lauren Sweester), for example. I feel as the film
goes on, and definitely in the book, you get the sense that Gail
came through. She made a choice, she is trying to live by it, and

yet you get the sense that their friendship is actually a salient and meaningful connection. They have a similar vantage point and they offer each other a huge amount of strength. In the book that was actually elaborated more, but we didn't have time. We actually filmed many of the scenes between Gail and Ree, but quite a few had to drop out because of time constraints in the film. But we really love that part of the story. It was hard—Gail used to have a bigger role.

W&H: Jennifer Lawrence as Ree was spectacular. How did that happen? How hard was it for you to get her to this place? I know she is from the South so that might have helped.

DG: It did. She was born and raised in Kentucky. And it helped at the audition so much because many of the young women had struggled with the accent and the dialect, and Jen had an ear for it. And I really enjoyed that she was not struggling. She did not have to use her psychic energy, her resources, to actually say a sentence. She wanted the role and made that known. That is always a huge thing, when an actor is able to communicate that she is really interested. And it is not so overt, but it is how they communicate with you and how they audition. She had read it and had taken it to heart and really felt like she could commit. And she did.

W&H: The film is bleak, like *Frozen River*. But you couldn't stop yourself from rooting deeply for Ree. And toward the end, it almost became a thriller. How do you achieve a balance with the bleakness of it but also really try to keep it uplifting?

DG: You just raised something interesting—we actually used *Frozen River* as a very positive role model. As an inspiration in the idea of . . . can this film be made? Who might like it? The very notion that this film is viable. And we were also pleased to see Melissa Leo bust out.

In a life with very limited resources, without any fat, it means that winter is going to be a struggle. Even in the world of fairytales, winter is always the setting when you show that the stakes are very high because survival is just that much harder. Everything is more dire—hunger, cold and what it takes to take care of two small kids in winter.

W&H: So this film's time period is heading into winter?

DG: Yes. In the Ozarks, they didn't have a severe winter the year we filmed. If we had filmed it this past winter, there would have been a huge amount of snow. They had very severe ice storms. But the trees were bare early. They're very exposed trees. They aren't like the weird symmetrical maples that we have on the East Coast. They were walnut trees that I always thought looked like nerve endings, the way they were splayed out. The fact is, in this case, the winter actually helped the story be even more vivid. When you build a fire for your siblings and you get near it and you are warm—it makes every human more warm. Also, Ree's ability to make the inside of her home safe for them becomes very palpable. Things are shown through a kind of starkness. In some ways, it's a tried and true way to bring a story to a vivid place.

W&H: I was thinking about Ree never having a childhood but being determined to give her siblings one. I'm thinking about the scene in the high school—she looks at it very longingly, knowing she doesn't have a chance.

DG: We know about that in urban settings, what it means to not finish school. I think the rural circumstances are a whole other area where not finishing high school can be a widespread issue. We actually tried to talk to people asking them to read that part of the script. Was it realistic? Would there have been intervention? Would she have been forced to stay in school? So, basically there is some sensitivity when people know someone's family is having a rough time. There is support. Olive branches are put out. There is an actual inquiry. There are benevolent teachers that seek out the student. And yet, if the student feels like it is impossible for her to finish for whatever reason, there is also this understanding that in some families it won't happen.

In those four states, Missouri and its neighboring states, education through military and employment through military has always been a viable link to resources. And with a war with an actual fighting army, that all shifted. What the recruiter (in the film) had to say to her was just so much more upsetting and complex.

W&H: **I couldn't believe this was a novel. It just felt so real. I want to talk a little bit about the drugs that have decimated so many communities. The awareness that the young people have about what the drugs have done to their entire family is so profound. Can you talk a little about the drugs and the influence of that?**

DG: Meth is so visible. Very early in life kids are such incredible observers. They know when an adult in their life is using, or misusing, or if they do something self-destructive, and there is an incredible feeling of helplessness. You want that adult to stop. Young people somehow want to intervene and they think they can do something but they can't. With meth—you don't miss it. There's just a mark of destruction on people that's just so visible. The evidence is so naked and flagrant. Kids see it.

W&H: **If you're not in school . . .**

DG: But the kids really do know. And there's a whole generation of children that were actually raised in houses where it was being produced. And that is where some very important and positive

intervention has been done because there is a legal basis to
remove and try to assist children, very dramatically and positively. Sometimes it is botched. It can destroy families. We met
a real Ree Dolly, a real seventeen-year-old girl who brought her
sixteen-year-old brother. They had been raised their whole life
in a house where meth was being made with a mom that was
really addicted. And she had a positive intervention. She and
her brother were being raised in a safe house. I was so happy.
And she said one thing that I thought was so remarkable that
I had never really heard. She said, all your life you are told you
can't speak up, that kids won't speak up. And it's not always
true. Kids will respond to intervention and they will speak up.
And she said that even as a young kid, she did believe there was
help out there.

W&H: **So this movie changed you?**

DG: I would say it's very hard to go somewhere very far away from
       your own home base and have to observe other people's lives
       and their life experiences, and not be changed. Just by the
       virtue of contrast. Even if you're just contrasting what you've
       known. As much as a filmmaker ever expresses curiosity about
       the so-called "other." I might ask the life models, the ones who
       helped us with the logistics of this film, a bazillion questions
       about hunting and what they eat and different things. They're
       equally curious about me.

       The thing is by working on a project far away, you end up
       asking a lot of questions about your own life. You are changed.
       It was relevant for me to ask myself why I have zero survival
       skills. People were surprised that I was so incapacitated in a
       rural setting. To see yourself as having one set of skills and
       reminding yourself that you don't have the other set of skills
       sometimes felt like a revelation. Had I had to fend for myself, I
       wouldn't have the skills in place to do that.

W&H: You've worked with Anne before and your DP Michael McDonough before. Is that correct?

DG: Yes.

W&H: So you have a cadre of collaborators. Is that really important to you?

DG: Yes. There are so many reversals of fate and luck in trying to get a film made. A burden shared is a burden made lighter. At first, a larger entity was going to get involved in the development of this project. That never came to fruition. The blow was serious. It was so close to the actual start of production, and we were literally defeated. Then we got this interesting form of cross-pollination. I would say, "Today I'm just feeling so pissed about this. Screw them." And Anne would say, "Yeah, screw them." And Michael said: "We don't need them. Let's make it for half the amount of money." So we got our fighting spirit back because we had each other's support; we said we would do it anyhow. You can't do that alone.

W&H: I think this film is going to have a long life. How do we get people to go see it? What's your message to people to get their butts in the seat?

DG: Not that many people have seen recent imagery of this part of the region. It's really rich and beautiful—the Ozarks. They maybe haven't heard recent music from there. The ballads are old. The treat for American audiences is to see two really hard-working American actors really give something.

W&H: Why don't we see more films with young female heroines?

DG: Basically, it's very hard to find female actors of value in this age range. We aged up for a while. We were looking at women who were twenty-four, twenty-five and twenty-six, thinking, "This is humiliating." Why do we live in a country where we have to ask a twenty-six-year-old woman, who is wonderful in her own right, to impersonate a seventeen-year-old? That doesn't seem right. There is room to let new people in, especially in this age range. But it wrecks the whole system, which is so rigid and hard to penetrate. We can blow someone up and if she has been in a film like *Juno*, then we can put her in four other films because we know what her value is now. But that doesn't leave room to discover someone who might come from the neighboring state, who has read it and can really feel it in her bones. What happens when you pick someone who doesn't already have a mark of worth on them? The same kind of logic applies to John Hawkes. Other names were always pushed at us.

W&H: **Kathryn Bigelow. She broke the glass ceiling this year. Can you comment on that?**

DG: I think what broke is the idea that women directors can tell stories that involve the life experiences of men. That they have some notes that they're taking, some observations, some understanding, some compassion, and some curiosities. Women can be seen as being interested in and qualified to tell these stories, and that therefore audiences could be more diverse. They would not be labeled so readily. Their films could be considered more of general interest.

The other thing that happens is that role models inspire role models. That's how history changes. There was a big role model right there. It was a good thing.

Marleen Gorris (DIRECTOR)
Nancy Larson (WRITER)
FILM TITLE: *Within the Whirlwind*

Date of Release (or festival premiere): November 5, 2009
(American Film Market)

Link to IMDb page: www.imdb.com/title/tt1142804

Link to Trailer: http://youtu.be/Y8Eytyo-DeU

BIOS: Marleen Gorris is an Academy Award-winning Dutch director. Her film, *Antonia's Line*, won the Oscar for Best Foreign Language Film in 1996, making her one of the few women directors to ever have won an Oscar. She studied English and drama, both in the Netherlands and England. Her films include: *A Question of Silence, Broken Mirrors, The Last Island, Tales of a Street, Mrs. Dalloway, The Luzhin Defence, Carolina, Livin' La Vida Loca*, and *Within the Whirlwind*.

Nancy Larson has written screenplays for a number of films, including *Coach, The Wizard of Loneliness, Isabelle Eberhardt*, and *Within the Whirlwind*.

DESCRIPTION: *Within the Whirlwind* tells the true story of Evgenia Ginzburg (Emily Watson), who was sentenced to ten years hard labor in Siberia during Stalin's reign in the Soviet Union. Watson is her usual wonderful self in this intense story about a woman who believes she was a solid and stalwart party member and winds up in a whirlwind of accusations with no power. But while the gulag is extraordinarily depressing, the film is a story of hope as Evgenia is able to find love with the camp's doctor (played by Ulrich Tukur) under these most difficult circumstances.

Interview Date: February 4, 2010

WOMEN AND HOLLYWOOD: **Nancy, tell us how the story began.**

NANCY LARSON: I had developed a film with another producer and the producer wanted to work with me again. And he asked me what book I would like to do. I had read this book [Evgenia Ginzburg's autobiography, *Within the Whirlwind*], and I said this is the one I would like to do.

W&H: **So they hired you to write the script?**

NL: I came in more like a writer/producer. I just wrote the script and the first person we thought of was Marleen.

W&H: **Marleen, what made you interested in the film?**

MARLEEN GORRIS: I was very interested in the subject because there is so little done about that particular period—the Stalin Purges and Stalin in general. And I was also fascinated with Russia. Even now, a great part of the population worships Stalin. So obviously the Russians did not do anything with their history in that sense, as for instance the Germans did. What I mean is that, in Germany, it came out into the open and people started talking about it and historians went into the subject. None of that happened in Russia. And then, of course, it was a personal story of a woman who had written very extensively with great memory about what she went through. Also I had admiration for this woman. Where does one get the power to survive something like this? I thought it would be fascinating to make a film about all these elements.

W&H: **Did you first think of Emily Watson? Had you worked with her before?**

MG: I can't remember when I thought of Emily. This film was very long in the making and the financing was difficult. First, we had a French producer and that went wrong. We ended up with a lovely German producer. And two countries, Poland and Belgium, supplied some of the money. But it took forever.

W&H: **When did you write the script?**

NL: I don't even remember. Must have been seven years ago. Of course, it was an ongoing process throughout the seven years.

W&H: **Do you feel that it was the subject matter that made it so difficult to finance? Is it that it was a woman's story? Is it a story about a time period that people would happily ignore and not pay attention to again?**

MG: You say this is a bio-pic, and they said "no bio-pics." When you say this is a political film, they said "no political films." They always came up with some excuse.

NL: There's always a reason not to make a film.

W&H: **Do you have distribution here in the United States? Are you looking for it? What are your thoughts for the next level for this film here in this country and elsewhere? Has it premiered elsewhere?**

MG: It has been shown elsewhere.

NL: In fact, it's been a work in progress. Between festivals there have been adjustments.

MG: One thing that didn't really work in our favor is the world crisis. Last year was abysmal. Half of the American distributors went broke and out of business. In Europe, it's not much better. We are looking for an American distributor. It's not exactly a barrel of laughs. It's either the big blockbusters that people go to or comedies, especially in bad times. But I presume that's part of the difficulty for a lot of independent films to find distributors.

W&H: **Most of your films have had a strong feminist theme. Has that been deliberate on your part?**

MG: I guess you could say so. I never really understood why it would be worth commenting on the fact that a film has a woman as a character. It still seems to be very unusual. Given the fact that more than half of the people on this earth are women, it should only be natural that we get this attention.

NL: It's funny, you don't say to a man, "I've noticed that you only make films about men."

W&H: **Do you feel that taking that position has helped your career? Hurt your career? Or is it just who you are?**

MG: Well, it is just who I am. It's difficult of course to say if it's hurt my career. I won an Oscar for *Antonia's Line,* which has a very feminist point of view. So I certainly can't complain about lack of attention. Of course, if I had made completely mainstream films or films lacking feminist perspective—then my career would certainly look different, I imagine.

W&H: **I understand that you directed an episode of *The L Word*? Was that fun? Enjoyable? How did you like working here in the United States?**

MG: I have worked in the United States before. I did a film called *Carolina* with Shirley MacLaine and Julia Stiles, which went straight to DVD because the Weinstein Company didn't like it enough. And the others were British. And they asked me one time. Actually, most of it was done in Vancouver, so I didn't really work in the States.

W&H: **Can you talk a little about the *Mrs. Dalloway* movie and your experience with that?**

MG: That also took years to make. It was really a wonderful experience with Vanessa Redgrave who is a magnificent actress. I actually shot the first part with the older people first. Then we had a break in the film because the producer lost all his money. Then the American distributors of *Antonia's Line* took over the film and gave me the money to finish it. And then I did the younger generation. That was very fortunate because that almost never happens that you break a film in the middle and then someone else gives you money to finish it. It was hugely enjoyable making a film like that.

W&H: **What is it like to be a woman director from a country where you can have a body of work?**

MG: The main difference is that women filmmakers, or any film-maker from a small country, are subsidized by the government. That is something that Denmark has, and Holland and Germany. In that sense it's easier. I think in Holland we have quite a number of women filmmakers even though there still aren't as many as men. But there is not such a strict differ-ence, as apparently there is in America. I did try at one time to make a film here in the States because I was asked and that didn't work out. And then of course you go onto other things. But it's tough. Whatever you do—it's tough.

W&H: **What is your advice for an upcoming and/or established screenwriter? And what is your advice for a director?**

NL: I have not had very good luck with the studios. I've had good luck in terms of getting many commissions but not in terms of getting films made. And I think you have to find a way. Europeans are more interested in what I do, so I tend to go there. They don't pay as much but they tend to make your films. But my advice is really to absolutely persevere with what you're truly interested in. Otherwise everything sounds alike.

MG: That is definitely my advice, as well. Persevere. Because what else can you do? Or choose a completely different profession all together.

W&H: **You come from a place where a woman's vision is treated differently. Is that true?**

MG: I don't know, I'm not so sure. My first films were met with a lot of opposition and also, fortunately, a lot of encouragement. But in many ways, I find the States freer. And almost every woman works in the States. But that's not the case with Holland, even though Holland is quite an emancipated country.

Courtney Hunt

FILM TITLE: *Frozen River*

Date of Release (or festival premiere): 2008 Sundance Film Festival

Link to IMDb page: www.imdb.com/title/tt0978759

Link to Site: www.sonyclassics.com/frozenriver

Link to Trailer: www.sonyclassics.com/frozenriver/trailer.html

BIO: Courtney Hunt made her feature film debut at the age of forty-four with the spectacular *Frozen River*. The film debuted at the 2008 Sundance Film Festival, where it was awarded the best feature. She holds a MFA in film from Columbia University, a law degree from Northeastern University, and a BA from Sarah Lawrence College. Her thesis short from Columbia, *Althea Faught*, sold to PBS and her second short, also entitled *Frozen River*, premiered in the New York Film Festival in 2004. Recently, Hunt was hired by Focus Features to write and direct the American remake of the French film, *Human Resources*. In addition, she will produce and direct her second original screenplay titled *Elfie Neary*, which takes place in 1904. She also directed episodes of the HBO series, *In Treatment*, starring Gabriel Byrne. She lives in Columbia County, New York, with her husband and daughter.

DESCRIPTION: *Frozen River* follows the story of two single working mothers who smuggle illegal immigrants across the Canada-America border to earn money. The film won the Grand Jury Prize at the 2008 Sundance Film Festival and was sold to Sony Pictures Classics. The film went on to receive critical acclaim and won the 2008 Gotham Award for Best Film, the Bronze Horse at the Stockholm Film Festival, and the Lena Sharp Award from the Seattle Film Festival, among others. The film was nominated for seven Independent Spirit Awards. And it also appeared on numerous top ten lists. In 2009, the film was nominated for two Academy Awards, including Best Original Screenplay for Hunt and Best Actress for Melissa Leo.

Interview Dates: August 1, 2008, and February 16, 2009.
(For the film and the DVD release)

WOMEN AND HOLLYWOOD: How did you get the idea for this film?

COURTNEY HUNT: This smuggling really goes on at the border three hundred miles from here [New York City]. It is a smuggling culture that has been around since Prohibition. The commodity may change—it has been booze and cigarettes—now it's illegal immigrants. I learned that women were involved and I went and met some of them in the late '90s. They were smuggling cigarettes at the time. They were really interesting. They happened to be Mohawk. That's how I came up with the idea.

W&H: **You are able to address race and class issues by putting a white woman with a Native American woman. Did you know that you wanted to have this cross-cultural conversation?**

CH: I did. One reason was a function of the storytelling. For us to understand the situation, we needed to see it through the eyes of someone who knew nothing about it. I did love this idea of a white woman and a Mohawk woman stuck in a car together and just seeing what happens.

W&H: **What compelled you to put pen to paper?**

CH: I wrote the first draft based on cigarette smuggling and wasn't happy with the way it came out. Then 9/11 happened, I had a baby, I moved upstate, and one day I was writing in my journal and this whole monologue of Ray's [Melissa Leo's character] just poured out. I thought it was a poem. And so I took that and it became the short film. Once I saw the short film got into the New York Film Festival and it got attention, I went back and said let's just show the whole thing.

W&H: **Did anyone say to you why don't you make this into a feature?**

CH: Nobody said they wanted to make it into a feature. Once I finished it, nobody said they wanted to produce or fund it.

W&H: **How did you find funders?**

CH: In other areas. I looked in real estate. I looked at areas where people had lots of profits.

W&H: **How much did it cost to make the film?**

CH: Well under a million dollars.

W&H: **It was purchased by Sony Pictures Classics after Sundance?**

CH: It was purchased before we won the award at Sundance.

W&H: **It is so hard nowadays for films from a female perspective to get made and released. Your film is resonating, and it's such a tough subject. Why do you think that is?**

CH: I think the reason is that it's a good story. It's a story with some suspense that grows out of the true motivations of the characters. I tell it in a really suspenseful way because that was the one commercial aspect of the movie that I could deliver to pay back my investors. And suspense makes you stay in your seat until the last frame because you need to see what happens to this woman.

W&H: **These two women initially don't like each other.**

CH: When I went to write, every day it would scare me that I was writing about two characters who don't like each other. I'd think: "Where can I go with this? Are they even going to speak to each other in the car?" I think that when we are around people from other cultures, especially when it's uncomfortable, we just want to flee. But they are stuck in the car together so they have to work it out. I like that the awkwardness that I was feeling writing it shows in the movie because that was the truth.

W&H: **How did you get Melissa Leo to be a part of this?**

CH: James Schamus—the head of Focus Features—brought *21 Grams* to the little town where I live and I met Melissa after I saw that movie. Her performance is really good in that film and I felt she had such a powerhouse persona and knew she could carry a feature. Most important, I thought she would be interested in the short based on the kind of character she played. Both Misty (Upham) and Melissa were in the short.

W&H: **Did you always know you were going to direct this piece?**

CH: Yes.

W&H: **Women directors find they have to write the scripts in order to get the directing gig. Has that been your experience?**

CH: Yes, it has.

W&H: **I've also interviewed women directors on their post Sundance experience. Some talk about the expectations out of Sundance. What were your expectations and what has been your experience?**

CH: I had high hopes and low expectations. I thought if I could sell this film, I will have succeeded beyond my wildest dreams. That was my goal and I really didn't worry about anything else. I didn't have an agent going in and I didn't worry about it. I had a sales agent but not an agent for me.

I sold my film and then I was done and ready to go home. Then we won the prize. And we won it from Quentin Tarantino. And it was so weird and so great. We had no idea that was going to happen. I remember walking past him at the directors' brunch thinking he is going to hate this movie. How wrong I was.

I had been working with this agent at William Morris, who was helping to sell the film, and they had given me a pitch, and I hired him as I walked off the stage. We went home to our little town and there was nothing. Then we went out to dinner and people just started coming up to the table because everybody knew, and that was sweet. Since then, I've just been reading scripts. I've had a charmed experience, first, that it's getting a release, and second, that it's getting a wide release.

W&H: So you are reading other people's scripts now? Are you going to write another script?

CH: I have one already written in a fourth draft and I'm going to do that, but I'd like to take a directing assignment first. I'm not particularly wed to my own work. I'm getting all these scripts to read and a book to adapt that they are going to pay me to do.

W&H: Are the scripts that you are getting mostly about women?

CH: No. I have one about a sheriff. They all have suspense. I feel that's really good, we are moving on.

W&H: Why do you think it's still so hard for women directors?

CH: There is a bunch of different elements to it. One is that it's just the pattern. You know when you are on an airplane and there is turbulence and the pilot gets on and says, "Hi, this is Captain Bonnie." And I think, "Bonnie, can she really do this?"

W&H: Do you really think that?

CH: I get a little nervous because I have the same biases as everyone else. I think it's just the matter of people getting used to the idea and getting familiar with it. Like with my crew, I'm sure when I first showed up they thought, "Oh my goodness, can she do this?" Then within three or four days, we are all on the same team.

The worst of it was my parents who said, "Do you really have to direct it?" This is coming from my mother who struggled her way through law school and I am like, "What? Yes I do." We have to: *a)* insist upon it; *b)* support each other; and *c)* be willing to be commercially viable. If suspense keeps me viable, then that's good. The next generation of men are totally comfortable seeing a woman protagonist as long as she's doing something. These relationship movies won't appeal to them.

You look at *Knocked Up* and all the Judd Apatow stuff. That's all about relationships. I find the characters more realistic. Everything doesn't have to be *va va va voom* in order to keep the male viewer watching. A woman engaged in fascinating action is just as interesting as a guy, in fact, more so, since we've seen guys pretty much do everything.

W&H: **The numbers of women directors are going backward not forward.**

CH: It's always going to be two steps forward, one step back. I feel that everything after 1979 has been going backward.

W&H: **Women I've interviewed bring up how Hillary Clinton was treated in the campaign in relation to their work as directors in Hollywood. Do you think that seeing a woman run for president could help propel more women into the director's chair?**

CH: I think it's about getting used to it, getting familiar with it, and realizing it's different from guys. It's different but not less than. I come out of law so I have this optimism because law is dominated by women at this point. At my law school, it was 60 percent women.

W&H: **Did you work as a lawyer?**

CH: No, but I finished law school and then went to film school. I worked for my husband as a lawyer doing murder appeals to pay for film school. Thirty or forty years ago, there were only a few women in law. Now it's not unusual to see a woman lawyer. I think that is one example of a once male-dominated world that is not at all anymore. There's plenty of room for everyone in that world, and I know it's going to be that way for film too because good stories are universal.

W&H: **Do you feel comfortable saying your age?**

CH: Oh yeah, forty-four.

W&H: **It's an awesome story that you directed your first film at forty-four. It's heartening.**

CH: I think, in a way, I have a little more credibility. It helps with the crew. It helps with the cast. It helps talking to the money dudes because they are not as scared and I am not as scared.

Part Two: February 16, 2009

W&H: **Talk a little bit about how things have changed for you since the premiere in Sundance.**

CH: I have access to better material, and many opportunities have popped up. There is a lot of interest from actors who want to work with me, and I'm having an easier time of getting something read. And I'm getting to pick and choose some different directing jobs, which is really nice. I've been hired for one that's a rewrite and I'm directing.

W&H: **I remember when we talked last time, you were very deliberate about wanting to not only write and direct, but wanting also to be a director for hire so that people could see you in both arenas.**

CH: Right. And I'm up for a job simply directing, a big job, which I can't name. Everything I'm offered is for directing. But sometimes there will be a rewrite, as well.

W&H: **That's incredible. You made this film for under $1 million, so are you looking at budgets in the $10 million range now, or lower since they know you can do an amazing movie on a million dollars?**

CH: People won't even talk about a million dollars. I made the
        movie for the better part of a million, but got it in the can for
        about half a million, and people just laugh when I tell them.
        They think that's a joke, that it's ridiculous. No one ever makes
        movies for that kind of money.

W&H: **Have you noticed the change in the audience due to the eco-
        nomic slowdown?**

CH: First of all, it's a strong story so people first talk about the story.
        But then the second and third things they used to talk about
        was mostly the smuggling. Now it's mostly the distress that
        they're in, economically, as people, as the situation described in
        the movie becomes less and less unusual.

W&H: **So it becomes more of a personal movie, whereas a year ago
        it was much more of a thriller with a situation that people
        couldn't see themselves being in.**

CH: I think there's a little more awareness that the people I'm
        writing about are not so far out there.

W&H: **Did you ever feel when you were writing that they were so far
        out there?**

CH: No. As soon as you leave any major city in this country, you
        run smack into people living in rural areas that may be eco-
        nomically forgotten, which is the truth about upstate New
        York. It's not just economically depressed, it's forgotten. And
        whenever you get into those communities many people live in
        trailers. It's a perfectly acceptable and normal thing to do.

W&H: **Talk about the reception overseas. Why do you think it's reso-
        nating for people outside the United States?**

CH: I'm surprised by the response, particularly in France and
        Spain. It's such an American film following the western model,

and I didn't know if it would translate and work with subtitles. And I was completely wrong. We had a huge reception in Spain and France. The box office in France is catching up with our U.S. box office and it's only been out for four weeks.

W&H: **And why do you think that is?**

CH: Well, there are many reasons. One of the reasons is that I think the distributor there is really hands-on. And I went to Paris and talked to many people. I used to live there so I'm familiar with the language. But more than that, I think it's just that there's this very intelligent film-going audience in France, and they go to independent films. They go to big films, too. And they have no problem with subtitles.

W&H: **And also, they have more of a history of women as leads, too, in those countries.**

CH: Yes. They're very happy with that.

W&H: **Can you elaborate more on a comparison I heard you make comparing Ray Eddy (Melissa Leo) to John Wayne and westerns?**

CH: Think of the classic American story venturing into lawless territory. A border is lawless territory. The Wild West was lawless and there was a sense that anything could happen. And that's sort of the feeling with *Frozen River*. These two women are in a space that doesn't have any law and order. So that's one big thing. And the other thing is just the style of John Wayne's acting, which I had recommended that Melissa [Leo] look to as a guide. John Wayne was really amazing at what he didn't do, and how much his lack of expression was really full of emotion.

W&H: **And you feel that when you look at Melissa Leo's face. I think it's so brave because so many actresses spend their time being** glossed up, and this is clearly the opposite of that. Talk a little bit about your goals for us seeing a real women's face.

CH: I took cues from movies like *Central Station* and *Alice Doesn't Live Here Anymore*. These were movies with real women in them. There are movies out there that start with a woman and they aren't glossy, they are real. She's in some sort of jeopardy and she needs to figure a way out. We follow her on that journey. In this role, she was willing to show a lot of pain. And you appreciate her flaws, as well as her acts of heroism. It's not like we're looking at her, it's like we're looking through her to what she's living.

W&H: I read what Quentin Tarantino said to you when he gave the Sundance award, "You put my heart in a vise and proceeded to twist that vise until the last frame." That is just an incredible quote.

CH: Yeah.

W&H: How did you create a real thriller—not a standard woman-in-peril type of thing?

CH: It wasn't really my intention to make a thriller. I just wanted to make something that you couldn't turn your head away from. So in doing that, I had to make sure that every moment was in pursuit of the goal, and that every moment involved the real dangers that they were facing. It's just that I'm showing it in a compacted ninety-seven minutes. There are people dealing with these kinds of dramas all the time that are just normal, everyday folks who often end up making very good decisions. And we don't really talk about that, because we want to have the big ending, and we want to cinematize it.

W&H: What's it like to have an Oscar nomination for your first movie? What was that moment like, when you heard you had an Oscar nomination for writing this movie?

CH: We watched it on TV at my house. My husband [Don Harwood, the executive producer] and I were so excited that Melissa had been nominated that we ran out of the room. And then we were like: "Oh, my God. We've got to go back and see what else has happened." And so we ran back in the room and that's was just when Forest Whitaker said my name and I just sank to my knees on the rug. It's an overwhelming and humbling experience.

W&H: **Your film was released in August, so there was the potential of just being overlooked during the awards season.**

CH: Right. The reason it's back around and it lasted has to do with, I think, the movie. But it also has to do with Michael Barker's (Sony Pictures Classics) faith in the movie, because it was a bold move to release in August. They had a lot of faith in the movie. So that was kind of cool for distributors, the first time around, to put that kind of faith in the movie. They were behind me. It's always been a tiny release. It's been in only like one hundred theaters. I think that people would go to it in multiplexes. It might take a minute to catch on, and that's the whole trick of the business, isn't it? You don't have a minute.

W&H: **No, you don't.**

CH: So that's the deal. Do I think that it could find an audience in the middle of this country? Yes, I do. And I think that it should and it deserves to, but will it? That's out of my hands.

W&H: **Why is it so hard for women directors to get noticed in the directing arena?**

CH: Here's my thing. I do not believe they're keeping us out. I believe when we want it bad enough we will get it. What I do know in my heart is that sometimes it's just a question of critical mass. But on the other hand, I had to make my own opportunity. And women are perfectly capable of making their own opportunities. I did it with no money and no nods of approval from virtually anyone. And yet I found talented, amazing people and put together a little crew and got it done.

W&H: **Do you think the freedom of not having been working with a studio and having raised the money on your own was essential to this process?**

CH: I do think that it had a big impact on it. Although now I'm meeting a lot of producers and I know that there are also producers out there who are distinctly gifted and who can really help you and be part of the creative process.

Photo Credit: Mark Hanauer

Callie Khouri

FILM TITLE: *Mad Money*

Date of Release (or festival premiere): January 18, 2008

Link to IMDb page: www.imdb.com/title/tt0951216

Link to Trailer: http://youtu.be/TotN5LX-9Uw

BIO: Callie Khouri galvanized women and sparked nationwide debate in 1991 with the hit movie *Thelma & Louise*, her screenwriting debut, for which she received an Academy Award. She was honored by the Writers Guild of America for Best Original Screenplay and won a Golden Globe Award and a PEN Literary Award. In 1992, she was recipient of the second annual Los Angeles Women Making History Award and the New York Women in Communications Matrix Award. *Glamour* magazine named her one of their top ten women of the year, as well. Her directorial debut was in June 2002 with *Divine Secrets of the Ya-Ya Sisterhood*, which she also adapted for the screen. Her second feature film is titled *Mad Money*. In 2006, Khouri collaborated with legendary television producer Steven Bochco to create an original television series for ABC/Touchstone entitled *Hollis and Rae*. She wrote and directed the pilot. Khouri serves as executive producer, creator, and writer for the television series *Nashville*, currently running on ABC.

Born in Texas and raised in Kentucky, Khouri attended Purdue University, where she majored in drama. She pursued additional training at the Lee Strasberg Institute in Los Angeles and later with Peggy Fuery. In 1985, she began working in film production, producing commercials and music videos. She currently resides in the Los Angeles area.

DESCRIPTION: *Mad Money*, a new comedy starring Diane Keaton, Queen Latifah, and Katie Holmes is about three women who conspire to steal money about to be shredded from the Federal Reserve in order to get their lives on track. Bridget (Keaton) is about to lose her home and her upper middle class dream, single mom Nina (Latifah) wants to get out of her bad neighborhood and get her sons into a better school, and Jackie (Holmes), well, she just wants a better trailer to live in. Bridget is the mastermind who comes up with the plan after being forced to get a job as a cleaner in the local Fed because that's the only thing she's qualified for after being out of the workforce for decades. She convinces the other ladies to go along with the plan and they are on the road (with lots of bumps along the way) to salvation.

Interview Date: January 16, 2008 (updated 2011)

WOMEN AND HOLLYWOOD: **2011 marks the twentieth anniversary of** *Thelma & Louise.* **Why do you think it has become such an enduring classic?**

CALLIE KHOURI: I can't believe it's been twenty years. I feel like it went by in the blink of an eye. It also feels like it was one hundred years ago. When I really think about it, for instance when I am speaking to a class, and I make myself go back to when I was writing it, I remember it vividly because writing it was such a powerful experience in my life.

W&H: **Where did you get the idea from?**

CK: From the great stream of ideas that just seems to be out there, and every so often you get to tap into it. I can't say it came from a specific incident or set of occurrences; it was just a strange accumulation of life experiences, feelings, and the desire to tell a story, but at the same time, it kind of had a life of its own. The idea, or the feeling of the idea, came fully formed.

W&H: **It was released at a time when it particularly resonated in our culture—we had the release of Susan Faludi's** *Backlash* **and the Anita Hill testimony. It became a cultural milestone.**

CK: Timing is everything.

W&H: **So where have we come as women onscreen in these twenty years, because it feels like we have never seen these types of characters again?**

CK: It's a strange thing. I thought this would really help. The response to this movie was overwhelming, both positive and negative. Looking back, you could say its impression was indelible. And yet, I can't point to a lot of other movies that have really followed in its footsteps.

W&H: **You could say that female characters have not progressed.**

CK: Well, there are more female action heroes. I know one of the things I was trying to do was to make characters that were unquestionably female in their thinking, but it wasn't about them being gender identified. They didn't have to change or do anything differently to be compelling main characters. It still seems like that women have to be powerful and *sexy*. As if, you can't be powerful without the sex. And that wasn't part of *Thelma & Louise*. Undeniably, Susan (Sarandon) and Geena (Davis) were, and are both incredibly sexy, but that wasn't what the movie was about. Angelina Jolie has been in several action movies but it has more often than not been cartoonish. It seems that movies that feature women as main characters deal mostly with the issue of family or their relationships.

Thelma & Louise was just about something different than that. I was putting them in a situation, which they didn't deal with in a certain way because of their gender, they just dealt with each situation as the characters would, not "as women."

Over the years when somebody asks me "as a woman," how do you feel about this; I think, I don't know what else to compare it to. As *this* woman I can tell you, but as *a* woman I don't know. I can tell you what I'm feeling, but there's another woman out there who is going to feel 180 degrees different. So there is not a specific thing that you can point to that 100 percent of women across the board feel about "x." It's every bit as broad and as varied as it is for men.

W&H: **After *Thelma & Louise*, your next job was *Something to Talk About*. What was it like writing that?**

CK: I would honestly say that because I had never written anything before *Thelma & Louise*, it was a struggle to figure out even how to do it. I didn't know *how to* write *Thelma & Louise* because I just did it. I wasn't being paid to do it by anybody. Nobody was waiting for the script. Nobody was expecting a certain type of story structure. And then I went right to work writing for a studio, and it was just a completely different experience and it took a lot longer. To say I was blocked is to understate it drastically. Part of it was all the stuff that was going on in the ether, as you mentioned. Barbara Boxer and Dianne Feinstein were running for Senate for the first time. I got to meet these unbelievably incredible women, all my idols. It was such an interesting time and my focus was not 100 percent on writing. And then, I was not really sure what I wanted to say next. I knew I didn't want to say the same thing over again. I thought it would be a challenge to write a movie that didn't have a gun in it. So that was a big part of the challenge of the next script because I thought, it is so easy when you have a gun in the action. What do you do when you don't have that? The kind of story you could tell still needs all the same emotional eruptions and explosions, but they have to be human, not mechanical. It just took me a while to figure out.

W&H: **How did you transition into directing?**

CK: It was a lot slower than I would have liked. When I wrote *Thelma & Louise,* I hoped to direct it. It was never my desire or my goal to be a screenwriter. I know *I am* a screenwriter and that's probably what I do better than anything else, but I enjoy directing a lot. I wanted to direct *Thelma & Louise* but more fortunate than getting the opportunity myself, was to have Ridley (Scott) want to do it. I can't imagine that I would have done a better job than he did, and who knows if the story would have had many of the qualities for which it is remembered. I also think it made a really great point to have a guy like Ridley take the script, direct it, and still have me be happy. It makes a point one way, and I hope it is starting to make the point the other way that the gender of the director is not the overriding, important thing. I think that Kathryn Bigelow has finally put to rest once and for all the question of whether a woman can direct a certain kind of picture. This gender identification with skills is misplaced.

W&H: **What's the difference for you between writing and directing?**

CK: It's vast. Writing is just a very solitary, arduous process and directing, although arduous, is first of all, a much more accelerated process. You have a certain amount of time to accomplish certain tasks and you are going to get it done. You have a lot of people helping you, and you are helping a whole lot of people make something actual out of something that has been either in someone's imagination, or a vision that is being shared by many more people now. So for me, it is just a lot more fun. I enjoy it so much. The worst day directing a movie is better than the best day doing almost anything else.

W&H: **The first movie you directed was based on a beloved book—** *The Divine Secrets of the Ya-Ya Sisterhood.* **How did that come about?**

CK: They just kept offering it to me. I don't know why I was resistant at first. I guess it was that I could just feel myself getting put into the box. I thought, "OK, the last thing I did was about these two sisters and now this is going to be about five women." I could just feel the nails being driven in to what I was going to get to do: stories about women. The thing that attracted me was not the soft and mushy part, but the dark and complicated parts of the story. Fortunately, they kept asking me and I finally said yes.

W&H: **You just illuminated one of the most difficult issues for women, which is the fact when we tell stories about women, we get put in a box. Whereas when you tell stories about men you are not in a box. How do we move beyond this?**

CK: I don't think it's just women that need to move beyond it, that's for sure. If a movie is female-centric or is about women, people—including women—don't think anything about adding the diminutive "chick flick" and rendering it insignificant. That phrase attaches all kinds of negative associations. A lot of times they are deserved. Honestly, I don't care if I ever see another wedding movie as long as I live. It's ridiculous. I understand why people get annoyed with them. I am annoyed by most of them. First of all, I haven't seen a truly great romantic comedy in years. Most of the romantic comedies now to me are just time off my life. Because they are going for a very specific demographic—the ones that are aimed at much younger women—it's all been done and it's boring me to tired sobs.

    But getting back to how we get women out of the box, a major problem is that the audience isn't demanding something else. Movies that are box office successes get remade over and over. Honestly, if I could answer it, I would. I threw the best pass I could, but nobody picked up the ball and ran with it.

W&H: **If people make money by putting women in a box, there is no impetus to change.**

CK: That's what audiences have come to expect. Do you think the studios or financiers care about the content of a movie? They want to know where they are going to be able to sell it, how much international appeal it will have. They could care less.

W&H: **I was wondering if *The Divine Secrets of the Ya-Ya Sisterhood* would be perceived differently now eight years later in terms of women's franchises.**

CK: Perhaps. I just had to watch it again not too long ago and honestly at the time it wasn't a movie where I was like, "Please let me make this movie, please let me make this movie." I have to say it was more of, "I want to be a director; this is what they are offering me. They are not offering me anything besides this." All the things that I was trying to get made were not getting made. It just came down to, "Do you want to direct? Here's the thing that they are going to let you direct. Go direct it." And that's what I did. And I did it to the best of my abilities and stayed true to the spirit if not the letter of the book as best I could. But still it's hard when you realize that you are being asked to do something that is going against all your instincts. I can't tell you the number of jobs that I haven't gotten because I directed that movie and also because people don't remember that *Thelma & Louise* wasn't a soft story. Most of them didn't see enough of the *Divine Secrets of the Ya-Ya Sisterhood* to know that it also wasn't really a soft story.

W&H: **People don't realize that *Thelma & Louise* wasn't a soft story?**

CK: Because the word "chick" is in their head, one of two things happen. They remember it as a "female bonding" picture, or they remember the two of them as murdering banshees, which is so nuts. They shot one guy and after that they blew up a truck and stole some stuff. It certainly wasn't *Pulp Fiction*. I've seen it referred to on more than one occasion as ultra violent. And wow, if that isn't a different standard for ultra violent I don't know what it is. It's strange.

W&H: **What attracted you to *Mad Money*?**

CK: First of all, I wanted to do a caper movie that was semi-plausible. It was based on something that actually happened. I just thought that it was fantastic that these women were so below the radar that nobody would have considered that they could have pulled off something like that. And they did it for years. I thought that was hilarious, and it was somewhat satisfying to say, "Here are these invisible women who nobody could believe were smart enough or wily or sophisticated enough to pull this off and they lived quite well for a number of years because of the blindness to them." They saw a hole in the system that others couldn't see, because they weren't down that low.

I thought the script that Glenn (Gers) did was really funny and once Diane Keaton and Queen Latifah and Katie Holmes were attached, I couldn't wait. I love Diane Keaton. Watching her work from *Annie Hall*, *Reds*, really everything that she's done. She's an incredible actress and I was thrilled to get to work with her. I also wanted to do something that was light, just for the fun of it. Something that was the opposite of a social statement, although as the economy crashed, it did have some relevance.

W&H: **The number of women directors are still staggeringly low. Do you have any thought on why this persists?**

CK: I have thoughts. I think it takes a long time to turn around a battleship. It's a hugely competitive business, still run almost entirely by men. It would be interesting to go back and look to see if women who have run studios have hired more women to direct pictures because you would think that would be where the change would come. But we should ask both the men and women who run studios if in this day and age, they can really make the case that women are less qualified. I certainly can't explain it. Perhaps it becomes a self-fulfilling prophecy—the people who aren't hired have less experience than those who are, and are therefore perceived as less qualified.

W&H: **Any advice that you would offer people in the screenwriting or directing area?**

CK: There's a lot of advice I would offer. The first thing I would say is get ready, because no matter how good you are, it is still going to be hard. It just doesn't matter. You might get an easy first one or second one but eventually you are going to be in the mud with everyone else, fighting to get what you want and you have to be in it for the long haul. And I've said it a million times—get ready to have your heart broken. Because it will be. But at the same time, when you get to do the thing you want to do, there is nothing more satisfying. I think that's true for anything whether you are trying to be a novelist or an actor or a musician. We are all just rolling the dice.

Kasi Lemmons

FILM TITLE: *Talk to Me*

Date of Release (or festival premiere): 2007 Cannes Film Festival

Link to IMDb Page: www.imdb.com/title/tt0796368

Link to Site: www.focusfeatures.com/focusfeatures/film/talk_to_me

Link to Trailer: www.focusfeatures.com/focusfeatures/film/talk_to_me

BIO: Kasi Lemmons's first feature-length film, *Eve's Bayou*, became the highest grossing independent film of 1997. The film won the Independent Spirit Award for Best First Feature and received seven NAACP Image Award nominations, including Best Picture. In addition, Lemmons received a special first-time director award, created just for her, from the National Board of Review. She also won the Director's Achievement Award at the 9th Annual Nortel Palm Springs Film Festival.

Kasi Lemmons's feature *Talk to Me*, starring Don Cheadle, was released nationwide in July 2007 by Focus Features to widespread critical acclaim. She received the 2008 NAACP Image Award for outstanding directing.

Lemmons is developing a film adaptation of the gospel musical *Black Nativity* for Fox Searchlight. She was also awarded a fellowship by the WGA and the Franco-American Film Fund to develop her script, *Strangers in Paris*, in France as part of the Autumn Stories project.

Lemmons has worked extensively as a mentor and educator. She attended New York University School of the Arts, UCLA, and The New School of Social Research Film Program. She resides in New York City with her husband and two children.

DESCRIPTION: At its heart, *Talk to Me* is a love story between two men. There's nothing romantic going on between the two lead characters, D.J. Petey Green (Don Cheadle) and Dewey Hughes (Chiwetel Ejiofor), but it is a love story nonetheless. Petey is an ex-con whose only ambition is to be on the radio. It's 1966, and Washington, D.C., is in the throes of the Civil Rights Movement. Petey manages to harangue Dewey into a job at the radio station where he works. Petey becomes a D.C. star because he is in the right place at the right time. He speaks honestly and openly about his life as a black man in a white world. Dewey has big dreams for Petey beyond the radio and their relationship unravels as he pushes him to heights he can't handle.

Interview Date: November 6, 2007

WOMEN AND HOLLYWOOD: **This film is a love story between two men, which is rarely seen on film. Why was it important for you to tell this story?**

KASI LEMMONS: One of the most important films for me growing up was *Butch Cassidy and the Sundance Kid,* which was a movie about male friendship. It helped shape my feelings about film relationships and I realized I didn't see that. I wanted to get inside a relationship between two men where they could be vulnerable and need each other. I feel that it's real, and yet men are very afraid of showing emotion and being demonstrative. It helps us to understand men more when we realize they are capable of these friendships.

W&H: **When did you know you wanted to make the switch to the directing chair? [Previously an actress, one prominent role Lemmons played was Jodie Foster's roommate in *Silence of the Lambs*.]**

KL: It happened very organically. It was the late '80s and I was into
        politics. I went to film school thinking I would put a camera on
        my shoulders and make documentaries. The first film I made
        was about being homeless in New York. But, I had a tendency
        to dramatize. Bill Cosby then hired me to write a screenplay
        (which was never produced) and that's how I got into the
        Writer's Guild.

        The storyteller part of me was always very alive. I wrote plays
        all the time. At a certain point, I had a story I could tell from
        the beginning to end and I realized I had to write it down. I
        wrote a part that I could play when I was forty. It happened
        faster than that. I met an agent and he said we had to put it
        together and find a director. People passed on it. One day I
        woke up and realized that I had to direct it (*Eve's Bayou*). I
        didn't suddenly decide that I was a director, and even after I
        directed *Eve's Bayou,* I thought I was done.

W&H: **It's unacceptable how few women and African American
        women directors there are working in film today.**

KL: In every other field, there are women. There are women in high
        levels of politics. There are women in high levels of manage-
        ment at the World Bank. There are women in high levels every-
        where. Why is it that there are not more women directors? It
        just doesn't make sense. It's a particular backward industry
        in this country. I can't speak for other countries because they
        seem better.

        Storytelling is not like running the World Bank. Storytelling
        has a masculine and feminine side. We're dealing with human-
        ity. As artists, women are wonderful at telling men's stories, as
        men have been wonderful at telling women's stories. Yet at the
        same time, you need the push and the pull. You need the other
        side of the coin.

W&H: **Why does this continue to be such a problem?**

KL: It doesn't make much sense that they wouldn't be interested in women's visions. Look at television. They are always looking for women's stories to tap. I think it might have something to do with the concept of what a director is—a white man, between thirty and fifty, with the hat on backward in sneakers with a little scruff.

W&H: **You lobbied for this film. Did you have to work harder to get this film?**

KL: I had to get the meeting. I had to wait until they had gone through meetings with the usual suspects. I made it known that I wanted to do the movie, and then, the only moment of self-consciousness I had was before the first meeting and it wasn't just that I was a woman. I went in super prepared and super passionate and I got through that meeting. I was halfway through my second meeting, and Mark Gordon said OK.

W&H: **Is this the same Mark Gordon who produces for TV?**

KL: He believes in the power of women. It's something he believes in and enjoys doing without thinking. It's not that he is making a political statement; it's just the guy he is. Mark saw my passion, heard what I had to say, and said OK.

W&H: **How important is it to tell African American stories?**

KL: It's very important, but there have been stories I have been attracted to that have not been African American stories. I've written all kinds of things; however I am attracted to characters. African American stories have such a dynamic history, and it's my people so it's special to me. I think we occupy an interesting place in American history—very violent, very strong, and triumphant—and so I am drawn to those characters. I am drawn to stories.

W&H: **What advice would you give a young woman director?**

KL: Find a way of telling a story that represents an aspect of you, so you can use it as a calling card to help shape your identity so someone else doesn't put you in a box. Create something or find a piece of material that is a love letter to yourself.

W&H: **What are you working on next?**

KL: I'm writing a pilot for Mark Gordon and CBS. I am also writing a piece for Picturehouse on the Civil Rights Movement.

Issa Lopéz

FILM TITLE: *Casi Divas*

Date of Release (or festival premiere): August 21, 2009 (U.S. release)

Link to IMDb Page: www.imdb.com/title/tt1049948

Link to Trailer: http://youtu.be/KzWd4fUkHCo

http://youtu.be/ftMzBR7QU-s

BIO: Issa López was born and raised in Mexico City. In 1995, she obtained a BA in Film Directing with a specialization in Screenwriting, from the Centro Universitario de Estudios Cinematográficos (Mexico's National University Film School). In 1996, she completed a two-year graduate program created by Televisa, (biggest broadcasting network in the Spanish-speaking world) to train writers for television, film, radio, and theater.

In 2003, she wrote the feature film *Ladies' Night*, which became the most successful Mexican film of the year and the fifth biggest top grossing Mexican film ever. In 2006, *Efectos Secundarios* (*Side Effects*), her first feature as a writer and director, became the second highest grossing Mexican film of the year. It received twelve nominations for the Diosa de

Plata Awards (the Mexican Film Press Award) and two nominations
for the Ariel, the Mexican Academy Award. It received a
Diosa de Plata award for Best Screenplay.

Her 2008 film, *Casi Divas* (*Road to Fame*), which she wrote and directed
for Columbia Pictures, was amongst the top three Mexican films released
that year. *Casi Divas* opened in the United States in August 2009.

DESCRIPTION: *Casi Divas* tells the story of four very different women vying in a contest to become the next big telenovela star. It is a story infused with dreams of changing your life and desires for celebrity and success. If you think the plot is all gloss, however, you will miss the real point of the film.

Francisca (Maya Zapata) is a poor Indian woman from Oaxaca who deals with race issues in the Mexican culture; Ximena Lizarraga (Ana Layevska) is a rich girl who has remade her body to fit into the culture but is miserable and really, really hungry; Catalina (Diana Garcia) works in the factories of Ciudad Juarez and uses her platform to raise awareness about young girls who continue to go missing in her community; and Yesenia (Daniela Schmidt) is struggling with issues of gender identity.

Interview Date: August 20, 2009

WOMEN AND HOLLYWOOD: Why were you drawn to writing and directing this story?

ISSA LOPÉZ: Two things were immediately very interesting to me. First, this global obsession with celebrity that plagues us. As if the simple fact of being on a screen, any screen, could wipe away all our worries. This need to become public, and being massively recognized, accepted, admired. As if the only true proof of our existence could be through celebrity. Second, the chance to portray the radically different ways to be a woman in Mexico. The radically different struggles that women face in a maddeningly contrasting nation. And the very different motives that can lie behind this search for the spotlight. From finding love to survival.

W&H: **You manage to make a fun story and infuse it with many important political issues including weight, class, gender, and race, as well as the important topic of young women who are kidnapped. Why was it important to include these elements and how were you able to keep it light while making sure that people really also thought about important issues?**

IL: This was the main challenge in *Casi Divas.* From the start, the producer of the film, Gabriel Ripstein, and I realized that if we were going to talk about young women in Mexico, we had to address these huge, vital issues. And in that case, could we bring such serious business to the Mexican middle class, a pop-consuming culture that goes for Hollywood fare, romantic comedies, and telenovelas? Because, that is your movie ticket buyer in Mexico. Could we make these issues the subject of coffee talk? We had to. It is increasingly urgent to bring the Mexican and Latino middle class, that decision-making group, to look at these issues. And the one way to do it was to make it entertaining, engaging, and fun, without taking the finger out of the wound. The way that I describe this movie is a cake with a blade inside. It was a constant fear and a very fine line to tread. So we worked together carefully on the script, on the casting, on the general tone, to keep this very fine balance.

W&H: **How did you get started in directing?**

IL: I attended film school and directing was my primary passion from the beginning. I had to learn to direct—writing has always been natural to me. But after film school I had to write telenovelas. Very few films were made in Mexico. Slowly and very painfully, I squeezed myself into filmmaking, in the beginning as a writer. I was successful as a writer, but I wanted to direct and it was very hard to convince an industry that has accepted and labeled you as a writer—or as anything, for that matter—that you can be something else. It's funny that these days, it's quite hard for me to sell a script without committing to direct it, too.

W&H: **This is a film done by a studio clearly trying to break into the Spanish-speaking market. What is the goal for the film in the United States?**

IL: I think we ended up with a movie that addresses Latino issues but also universal ones. We've had very powerful responses from Latino and non-Latino audiences. Right now, its core target is the Latino community. But I believe that celebrity obsession, media manipulation, abuse of women, racism, and above all, women dreaming, can appeal to all audiences.

W&H: **What are you doing next?**

IL: I am both writing a comedy for the United States and a comedy for Mexico, with Gabriel Ripstein, who I worked with on *Casi Divas*. The one for the United States is about men. The one for Mexico, about women. Let's see which one moves faster!

W&H: **What type of advice would you offer a female writer and director in the business?**

IL: To be incredibly stubborn. If you are doing this, it is because you believe you have something to say. And if that's the case, stay put until you've said it.

Angelina Maccarone

FILM TITLE: *Vivere*

Date of Release (or festival premiere): 2007 Tribeca Film Festival

Link to IMDb page: www.imdb.com/title/tt0497467

Link to Trailer: http://youtu.be/7T5iG-xJP-k

BIO: Angelina Maccarone started out as songwriter before she wrote and co-directed her first feature film, *Kommt Mausi Raus?!*. Other films are *Alles Wird Gut (Everything Will Be Fine)* and *Ein Engel Schlagt Zuruck/Helgoland Babylon (An Angel's Revenge)*. Both films were for German public television and were also successful on the international festival circuit.

Fremde Haut (Unveiled) was in competition at the Karlovy Vary Film Festival and won the Hessian Film Award in 2005. She was awarded the Golden Leopard at the Locarno Film Festival in 2006 for *Verfolgt/Hounded (Punish Me)*.

Between 2007 and 2009, Maccarone wrote and directed three episodes for the German cult-crime classic *Tatort*. Her film *Vivere* premiered at the 2007 Tribeca Film Festival, and won the award for Outstanding Artistic Achievement at L.A.'s Outfest. She branched out into documentaries with the 2011 film *Charlotte Rampling: The Look*.

DESCRIPTION: *Vivere* takes place on Christmas Eve in a dreary town outside Cologne, Germany. Three women of different generations—two sisters and a mysterious older woman—are on the run from their lives, and each is affected by the other women in her journey toward creating her future.

Francesca (Esther Zimmering) has been driving a cab for years to support her sister, Antonietta (Kim Schnitzer), and their father. When Antoinetta takes off for Rotterdam with her musician boyfriend, Francesca goes in search of her. On her journey she encounters Gerlinde (Hannelore Elsner), and they form an unlikely team in the search for Antoinetta.

The story is told from each woman's individual perspective. When the stories converge at the end, the three have come together for one another, and you get a glimmer that maybe they have created some new connections to one another that will help each of them on her next journey.

Interview Date: February 27, 2008

WOMEN AND HOLLYWOOD: You are the writer and director of this film. How did you come up with the idea for the film, and did you write it with the intention that you would direct it?

ANGELINA MACCARONE: Since I am a writer/director as you said, I did write *Vivere* with the intention to direct it, as well. In this case, it is an important part of the film since the way it is shot is intertwined with my intention of showing three different views of basically the same events and thus making it the subjective story of each of the three protagonists. The basic idea was to show three women of different generations who are at some crossroads in their lives. They all have to make a seemingly small decision that will have great impact onto their lives.

W&H: **Explain the title, *Vivere*.**

AM: *Vivere* is Italian and means "to live." The three women are in a kind of waiting situation. They wait for other people to make decisions and to tell them what to do. In order to take their lives into their own hands and responsibility, they have to give up their waiting and just decide that life begins NOW.

W&H: **Each of the women in the film is lonely and desperate to make a connection to others around them. What is the message behind the desperation of people to connect?**

AM: I believe that we as human beings are not self-sufficient. But still, we need to grow up in the sense of becoming responsible and emotionally independent to be able to have deep and meaningful relationships that are not based on need in the first place. This sounds like a paradox—becoming independent in order to be able to belong—but this is how life works, I guess, with paradoxes.

W&H: **What do you want people to get out of the film?**

AM: I hope for people to think about their situation, their wishes, and maybe make them take the first step into the direction they want to head into. Every small step takes you further. I hope this comes across while watching the characters on screen.

W&H: **Your film is not only written and directed by a woman, it stars three women, and it is produced by a woman. That is very uncommon in the United States. Is it easier for women writers and directors in Germany, and what can the U.S. industry learn about how to integrate more women's visions and stories into the film business?**

AM: I know too little about the movie business in the United States, but in Germany, it is not necessarily easier for women. We worked on the funding for this film for nearly ten years. Maybe this was due to the fact that there are three female main characters. But still, it was great fun working with Anita, the producer, and the cast: Hannelore, Esther, and Kim.

Adriana Maggs

Date of Release (or Festival Premiere): 2010 Sundance Film Festival

Link to IMDb Page: www.imdb.com/title/tt1397502

Link to Film Site: www.grownupmoviestar.com

Link to Trailer: www.grownupmoviestar.com

BIO: Adriana Maggs is the executive producer, co-creator, and head writer of the Gemini Winning series *Three Chords From the Truth*. Adriana has most recently written on the TMN series *Call Me Fitz* starring Jason Priestley. She was the head writer on *The Wilkinson's* and wrote the episode that garnered the Gemini Award for best individual performance in a comedy. Adriana won awards in Canada for her two short films including the Outstanding Writer's award at the Atlantic Film Festival in 2004. She created the series *Rabbittown* for CBC with Sherry White and was a contributing writer and actor in the award winning series *Hatching, Matching and Dispatching* for CBC. She wrote and directed *Grown Up Movie Star*, her first feature film. (Credit: *Grown Up Movie Star* Official Site)

DESCRIPTION: *Grown Up Movie Star* tells the story of disgraced NHL star Ray, and his precocious daughters, Ruby and Rose. Once the town hero, Ray has returned home to Newfoundland from the United States following a drug conviction, only to have his wife, Lillian, leave him for another man and aspirations of stardom. With Lillian gone, Ray flails from woman to woman trying to find a replacement for her, while struggling against a growing awareness of his homosexuality. At loose ends for lack of guidance, Ruby attempts to follow her mother's starlet dreams with makeup and sexual behavior, and in a desperate plea for attention, begins putting herself in increasingly risky situations. Ruby begins spending more and more time with Ray's best friend, Stuart, confined to a wheelchair following an accident involving Ray. When Stuart finds himself attracted to Ruby, dangerously motivated by fear and anger, he leads the three of them toward a heartbreaking conclusion. (Credit: *Grown Up Movie Star* Official Site)

Interview Date: January 28, 2010

WOMEN AND HOLLYWOOD: **How did you come up with the story for**
** *Grown Up Movie Star*?**

ADRIANA MAGGS: *Grown Up Movie Star* was a short film script I
  wrote and was work-shopping on a panel. A local producer, Jill
  Knox-Gosse, was interested in it and asked me if I would tell
  more of the story and make it into a feature. The characters
  and scenarios are rooted in the themes that I explore both in
  my work and in my life.

W&H: **Female directors tend to get pigeonholed into certain types of**
  movies. Are you aware of that, and did you ever take that into
  consideration when writing this film?

AM: No, I didn't take that into consideration. I come from a place
  that is completely open to artists, a community that fully

supports all storytelling perspectives. I actually find it really hard when I step onto a "main stage," so to speak, that so many women artists and filmmakers struggle to have their stories told. But I am not naive to think that the support we receive from the Newfoundland government and arts community is "standard" practice. I am so thankful to have been nurtured in a creative environment. But after having moved to Toronto, I do understand the importance of supporting women in the arts and appreciate all the strong and talented filmmakers and producers who as women have really paved the way for the rest of us. Heather Rae, producer of *Frozen River*, comes to mind.

W&H: **Do you think it's easier for a female director to be more successful in directing if she also writes the film?**

AM: Again, I'm finding the question unusual, considering how I was, if you will, raised in a community of artists. I suppose it's easier for a first-time director, whether male or female, to have an opportunity to direct if they, in fact, write their own script. I really want to believe that good storytelling is good storytelling, and I also feel watching a film is like going to an art gallery or reading poetry or any artistic medium. The view is subjective, based on taste, life experiences, tolerance, empathy, and they will choose whether they like or dislike a film based on individual taste whether written and directed by a woman or a man.

W&H: **What does getting into Sundance mean for your film and your career and what are you hoping to get out of it?**

AM: It is a complete honor and really wonderful to have *Grown Up Movie Star* included in such a prestigious and welcoming festival. I have always thought that if I could have a film in a festival, I would have wanted it at Sundance. The history of the

festival, the amazing support of independent film and filmmakers, the amazing Sundance Institute are all reasons I am
very proud our film was accepted this year.

Once I wrote the film and we were on set, it became everyone's
film. The actors—Shawn, Tatiana, Jonny—and the amazing
crew really brought it to life and added so much to the story.
They really let me see the film through new eyes and it was like
discovering the story all over again. So what am I hoping to
get out of it? Well, I am really happy people are coming to see
our work; I hope that people appreciate the work and hope that
some can relate to the characters and their personal struggles.
And being from a small island off the coast of Canada and
arriving in Park City on an international stage, I am excited to
meet other filmmakers, see lots of films, and figure out a way
for more people to see ours!

W&H: **The film tells the story of a man who comes to terms with his
sexuality and a girl beginning to understand her own. Talk a
little bit about how you handled those situations.**

AM: Just from places of truth. I believe we all struggle with our
sexuality at some point in our lives. As young women, we are
constantly bombarded with images, celebrities, music, and
tremendous pressure to be more than we are at any age. Not
to mention the obvious struggles for young men as they see
young women as objects of desire. As far as Ray is concerned,
he's really about love and finding his way. Being a good dad,
son, and finding peace and living his own truth. Their journeys
are paralleled because it's a big time in both of their lives.

W&H: **Homophobia in sports is still such a huge issue, especially
here in the States where so few athletes have come out when
they were playing professionally. Why did you add that element to the story?**

AM: I wanted to look at fear, not just from a female perspective but sexuality in its ultimate fear-based place, and pro sports and celebrity seemed right. It's not really that Ray is a gay, professional athlete. It's that Ray is a small town boy, who was a small town hero that messed up, lived a lie and now is trying to find the freedom to live life on his own terms. But I'm not denying that being socialized in hockey or a macho sport that begs hetero machismo is a horrible place to be gay. Homophobia is alive and well everywhere no matter what we think. I just wanted to gently address love and desire between two people and living life in your own truth.

W&H: **What advice do you have for budding female writers and directors?**

AM: Just to do it. Write what you feel and be who you are and stay true to your stories no matter what people say or where you are from. I really hope one day that we'll all just be filmmakers and not qualified by our genders, age, race, but remember, I'm from a small island off the coast of Canada that has a utopic approach to supporting artists.

Photo Credit: Susan Shacter

Jodie Markell

TITLE: *The Loss of the Teardrop Diamond*

Date of Release (or festival premiere): 2008 Toronto Film Festival

Link to IMDb page: www.imdb.com/title/tt0896031

Link to Site: www.teardropdiamond.com/home.html

Link to Trailer: www.teardropdiamond.com/home.html

BIO: Born and raised in Memphis, Tennessee, Jodie Markell studied theater from an early age and eventually attended Northwestern University. After moving to New York, Markell studied at Circle-in-the-Square Theater. As an actress, Markell has been featured in films by directors including Woody Allen, Jim Jarmusch, Todd Haynes, and Barry Levinson. On television, she played a recurring role on HBO's *Big Love*. She has also appeared in *Law & Order* and *The Good Wife*.

Markell adapted and directed the award-winning short film, "*Why I Live at the P.O.,*" based on Pulitzer Prize writer Eudora Welty's classic story. The film premiered at the Seattle International Film Festival/Women in Cinema, and has played at numerous festivals since, including the New Orleans Film Festival, where the film was awarded the Moviemaker Magazine Breakthrough Award. The film was screened at the National Museum of Women In The Arts in Washington, D.C.

Markell's feature film directing debut is Tennessee Williams' *The Loss of a Teardrop Diamond*, which premiered at the Toronto International Film Festival.

DESCRIPTION: Tennessee Williams had a serious knack for writing about Southern women who just couldn't fit into the culture, who were stultified and driven mad when the constrictions of their world closed in on them. Bryce Dallas Howard is Fisher Willow, the latest Williams incarnation in the newly-discovered script that Williams wrote directly for the screen, *The Loss of the Teardrop Diamond*.

Willow is an interesting young woman who tries to play by the rules of 1920s New Orleans, but simultaneously chafes at those same rules. She doesn't fit in and wants to get the hell out, all the while knowing she's stuck.

The Loss of the Teardrop Diamond also includes performances by Ellen Burstyn as a woman who wants to die with dignity; Mamie Gummer; and a brief cameo by Ann Margaret.

Interview Date: January 5, 2010

WOMEN AND HOLLYWOOD: **Why did you want to make your directing debut with this screenplay? Tennessee Williams is a lot of
pressure even for an experienced director. But you took him
on your first time out of the gate. Why?**

JODIE MARKELL: When I was fifteen, growing up in Memphis,
Tennessee, I was cast as Laura Wingfield in a high school production of *The Glass Menagerie*. By the time I was seventeen,
I had read everything by Williams that I could find, and I had
also been inspired by Elia Kazan's classic films, *A Streetcar
Named Desire*, and my favorite, *Baby Doll*. Later, as a young
actress, in New York City, I saw a number of productions that
did not feel organic to the Southern sensibility that I knew.

I wanted to reclaim Williams and bring his visually poetic
world to the screen in a fresh way with as much vibrancy and
authenticity as I could achieve in the hope of inspiring a new
audience to rediscover this original American voice. I never
thought of it as choosing material for my first time out of the
gate. I simply thought that this screenplay needed to be realized and the connection I felt to the material made it the right
project for me to pursue.

W&H: **In the production notes you said, "I instantly sparked to
Fisher Willow and related to her as a strong female character
in the Williams mold." Can you elaborate further?**

JM: As a teenager with artistic tendencies who often felt a bit
different, I had an affinity for Williams' sensitive characters
who are searching for something authentic in a harsh world.
Fisher Willow is a young woman struggling to find her voice
and trying to understand how to connect with someone
she loves in a genuine way. I related to Fisher's longing to be

understood in a conventional society. Fisher says, "I am out of my element here." I think she is not only speaking for Williams himself, but for anyone who marches to the beat of a different drummer. She says, "I want to be with people who do things—paint, write, compose music, and so forth . . ."—I know how she feels, that's why I moved to New York.

W&H: **Why do you think that Tennessee Williams was able to write such brilliant yet flawed women in a truly unique way?**

JM: Williams said he never wrote about a vice that he had not observed in himself. I think there is a part of him in all his characters. And he always had a tendency to look at the more sensitive side of things. He started out as a poet after all. He also had several women amongst his close friends and family that were, as you say, "brilliant yet flawed"—especially his mother and his sister Rose who inspired many of his characters. He often wrote about women who were too beautiful, too romantic, too sincere, too sensuous, and too witty to be understood by a society that did not prize women for being smart or adventurous in spirit. I think he perhaps held the belief that being human means that we are naturally flawed even though conventional society believes that everyone should be flawless, fit in perfectly with what is expected, and not make any waves.

W&H: **What were the biggest challenges in making this film?**

JM: Before arriving in Louisiana, Giles Nuttgens, our cinematographer, said a period film usually requires a minimum of four months. But we were faced with the challenge of bringing scope to Williams' world despite the indie budget and our twenty-eight-day shooting schedule. And yet, I actually believe that this kind of challenge comes with the territory of independent filmmaking and forces filmmakers to work efficiently, be resourceful, and make creative choices in a courageous way.

W&H: **Talk about the difference between acting and directing. Do
         you want to direct more?**

JM: As an actor, after researching, creating, and becoming the
         character, probably your most important goal is to be in
         the moment. As a director, one of your goals is to create an
         environment of trust and support so that the actors can make
         discoveries as they work. It is those discoveries that light up the
         screen. While keeping the creative vision in mind, the director
         has to wear a lot of hats, run the set, and put out a lot of fires.
         The director also has to think of how each moment works in
         relation to the whole vision—from shooting to editing to the
         final print. The director has to think in the past, present, and
         future—all at once—whereas the actor gets to be more in the
         present. But in both acting and directing, it is really all about
         finding the truth in each moment and sharing that with an
         audience.

         I will continue to work as an actor and director in both theater
         and film because I think what you learn in one discipline
         informs the other. But right now, I am looking forward to my
         next film as a director. I have several projects in development
         and am reading scripts, as well.

W&H: **What do you want the audience to be thinking about when
         they leave the theater?**

JM: I want the audience to feel that they have experienced
         Williams' words and his world in a new way. I want them to be
         touched by the honesty in two young people's search for some-
         thing real and their longing to connect. I want them to con-
         sider how difficult and how rare it is to really "see" and really
         "hear" another human being. And most of all, I want them to
         have their own experience and their own response to the film
         that I have no way of predicting. Making a film is kind of like

raising a kid and then sending her off to college; you have to let go and realize that your film is going to be having all kinds of encounters with all kinds of people that you will never know and that you have no control over.

W&H: **What advice do you have for other female filmmakers?**

JM: Stop defining yourself as a female filmmaker and just think of yourself as someone who has a story to tell and the skills and the life experience to tell it. Look for material that speaks to you, and then find a producer who believes in the material as much as you do. Every now and then someone says to me, "Do you realize that you are the first woman to direct a major Tennessee Williams film?" I really never thought of it that way; I just thought I had a certain understanding of how to tell this story.

Photo Credit: Petra Nettelbeck

Sandra Nettelbeck

FILM TITLE: *Helen*

Date of Release (or festival premiere): 2009 Sundance Film Festival

Link to IMDb Page: www.imdb.com/title/tt1012729

Link to Site: www.helenmovie.com

Link to Trailer: www.helenmovie.com

BIO: Sandra Nettelbeck was born in Hamburg, Germany, and studied film production at San Francisco State University. After leaving the United States, she worked as a TV journalist in Hamburg before she moved to Berlin to make her feature-length TV movie debut, *Loose Ends*, in 1995. In 2001, she made her theatrical feature debut with *Mostly Martha*, followed by her second feature, *Sergeant Pepper*, in 2004. *Helen* is the fifth feature-length film she has written and directed. It is also her first English-language feature. She is currently in post-production with her second international feature, *Mr. Morgan's Last Love*, an adaptation of a French novel, with Michael Caine, Clemence Poesy, and Jane Alexander. After several years of shuttling between Berlin, Bordeaux, and Los Angeles, Nettelbeck now calls Berlin her permanent home.

DESCRIPTION: *Helen* is the story of an accomplished professor, played by Ashley Judd, who has to acknowledge and reconcile her clinical depression. Helen does not want to share this painful secret, but if she doesn't, it just might destroy her. Eighteen months after its premiere at Sundance, *Helen* finally received a limited release in New York and DVD.

Interview Date: July 30, 2010

WOMEN AND HOLLYWOOD: **In the press notes, you talk about how you were inspired by your friend's suicide to tell this story. Why did you work so hard and long (ten years) to get this film made?**

SANDRA NETTELBECK: I was profoundly shaken by the death of my friend. The terrible loss, the painful questions and self-doubt that inevitably come with such an experience stayed with me. But it wasn't until three years later, when I read an article in *The New Yorker* by Andrew Solomon, about his battle with and survival of his own depression, that I started working on *Helen*. Andrew's story of survival inspired the story of *Helen*, and I felt it was a hugely important story to tell. So many people are affected by this deadly illness, and we still know so little about it. I am convinced that the lack of information, support, and acceptance that clouds clinical depression costs lives every day. I wanted to do my part in trying to change that. This kind of motivation, to feel that you have something to say that will matter, make a difference, and possibly help other people goes a very long way.

W&H: **Mental illness is a very common theme in films, yet we usually see other people commenting on the person who is ill. Here you give us almost an x-ray of a person living with depression. Why was that important to you?**

SN: It was important to me to try and tell the story from Helen's perspective. We've seen plenty of films about mental illness, addiction, etc., from the perspective of the husbands, wives, parents, children, and friends about their experience when a loved one falls ill. I wasn't interested in that, even though the family plays a crucial role in *Helen*. I wanted to show what it is like on the inside of depression. Shed a light on the enigma of a hellish disease and the extent to which it can ruin us. Depression, by nature, is the loss of communication. Film is all about communication. That is a tricky opposition to balance throughout a two-hour drama. I hope that I managed to give a glimpse of what it can be like to live in such a skin. I wanted to give the audience an idea of what it feels like when these walls are closing in on you.

W&H: **This is not an easy movie to watch, but it is hopeful and redemptive. What can you say to people who might be put off and not want to make the effort to see a "hard" movie, especially in the summer.**

SN: It may be even harder to watch it in the winter! No, seriously, this is a tough movie in any weather. And I'm sure it's not for everyone. But in ten years, I have not met one person who was not in some way directly or indirectly affected by this illness. Everyone has a story to tell. Consider the numbers for a moment. In the United States alone, almost twenty million people suffer from depression, more than twice as many women as men, and it is the leading cause of disability in the country. And these are just the ones we know about, the ones who got treatment, who managed to face the fact that they needed help.

But *Helen* is also, first and foremost, a love story. It asks the question that I always ask, and that really is the one question that I never get tired of asking—what love can do for us. *Helen* gives a big answer to that. No matter how hard or dark it gets, I know there is hope and love, and I think the movie compounds that. How crucial it is not to give up hope, under any circumstance. Not as the one afflicted, nor as the one trying to help. I've met many people who shook my hand after the movie because they either finally felt understood or did understand in a way they hadn't before. So I do believe this film can make a difference. And to me as a filmmaker, that is my proudest moment.

W&H: **How did you get Ashley Judd?**

SN: Actually, she got to me. Somebody gave her the script to read and she wrote me a passionate letter about how much it would mean to her to be involved in this film. What she hadn't been told was that, at the time, I already had a lead actress committed to the project. Ashley and I met anyway because I was very moved by her conviction and enthusiasm, her readiness to take on such a challenge. A few months later, fate would have it that my lead actress had to leave the project due to a prior commitment and ill timing. So I called Ashley and asked her if she would still consider the role. She said yes right away, and luckily for me, she was available. I think it was meant to be. The film was as personal to her as it was to me.

W&H: **Ashley Judd goes to depths we have never seen from her before. How were you able to get such a stark and brutally honest performance from her?**

SN: Ashley was ready and prepared to give herself to this complex and difficult performance in a way that doesn't happen very often. I think that is the greatest gift to any director—when it is as meaningful and significant to an actor to embody a character, become part of a story, as it was for Ashley to portray Helen. Of course, it is also a huge challenge. How much do you push someone on this journey, and how do you protect them? I had to rely on Ashley to draw the line, all I could do is offer her my guidance, my presence, a safe haven any time she needed it—and ask her to trust me as a director. I think she is a brilliant actress, and what she is able and willing to share with us on the screen as Helen is nothing less than extraordinary.

W&H: **There are two different forms of mental illness dealt with in the film—depression, which Ashley Judd's character suffers from, and bi-polar disorder, which Lauren Lee Smith's character, Mathilda, suffers from. How were you able to choreograph the scenes between the two actresses who were both dealing with very different emotions that needed to come out onscreen?**

SN: As a director, I do everything to make the actors feel safe, and if they trust me, they can go to places they haven't been to before. There is also something truly intimate about Lauren Lee Smith's performance, something very private and raw. I don't think you get that if the actors don't believe you'll do right by them or if they're not convinced that you know what you're doing, that you will protect and appreciate what they give you. I think both Ashley and Lauren felt extremely self-confident inside of their roles, and I myself had very precise ideas about each of the characters that I was able to convey to the actors. So nobody got lost. I think it was this clarity that guided us through the scenes. There was never any doubt in my mind about their relationship, how they affect, oppose, care for, and love each other for who they are. The very thing that drives the two women together, their ability to accept each other and give each other the space (and company) they need, their unique relationship within the story, their dynamic opposition and alliance is also what makes the scenes work, and ultimately how Ashley and Lauren worked next to each other. And even though they deal with different illnesses, Mathilda knows depression, as it is part of her condition. She knows how Helen feels, and this is their common ground. Helen on the other hand doesn't know mania; she can't follow Mathilda to that place. She doesn't understand the terrifyingly appealing ambivalence of bi-polar disorder that Mathilda feels and lives with, and that is precisely where she loses her.

W&H: **Depression and mental illness in general is pervasive yet is still stigmatized. The most fully functioning person could all of a sudden be plunged into such deep depths. What do you want people to learn from this film?**

SN: That it can happen to everyone. That it often happens to people you least expect it of. Also, of course, and this is particularly challenging, people have to understand the fine and fluctuating line between unhappiness and illness. That people, including and especially the sick ones, often can't tell the difference— sometimes until it's too late. Many people would never get as sick as they do if they would find help sooner. The stigma is everywhere, maybe even, or particularly, in the hearts and minds of the people who are ill. You very often hear severely depressed people wish they had cancer, broken bones, anything other than depression—in other words, a "real" illness. Something one can see, point to, identify, isolate. Depression is invisible, often masked (by alcoholism, for example), and it afflicts the mind, so it robs us of the very organ we need to cope with it in the first place. It can be a deadly cycle. When you're inside the illness, you not only lose your grasp of reality of perspective and hope, you also lose your ability to understand and rationalize your condition. Death becomes attractive because it seems to be the only means to heal the disease.

What I want people to learn above all else is that there is no shame in seeking help and that the best help one can offer as a loved one or friend is to help a depressed person find that help. Nobody expects people with diabetes to "pull themselves together" and try living without the insulin. But there are many people who would still be alive today if they had found the proper professional help at the right time, and this includes medication. I do think we have a lot to learn and I could go on and on. If I had to sum it up, once again, I'd say, don't be afraid or ashamed to ask for help, don't give up hope, and don't give up the fight.

W&H: **You also really try to get to the heart of how mental illness is so misunderstood. When Helen's husband David (played by Goran Visnjic) says to her psychiatrist, "Helen is unhappy," the doctor responds, "Your wife is not unhappy; she is ill." Can you talk about how hard it is for people to understand mental illness?**

SN: It's a bitch. As I said, we can't point to it. Multiple sclerosis doesn't look like a broken heart. Cancer doesn't feel like sadness. Clinical depression, however, moves within this realm.

And we're inclined to solve our own problems, get a handle on things, tough it out, move on, take control, be a winner, not whine, etc. Even when depression is at its worst—when your despair is beyond belief, when you can't get out of bed, when you feel nauseated all the time, when you can't sleep, when you loathe yourself inside and out, when nothing makes sense and you don't feel love for anything, when you can't stop crying and all you can think about is how best to end your life—even then, the idea that it is your fault, that you really only need to pull yourself together and you would get better, can easily manifest itself. And it's not surprising. The lines are almost impossible to draw, and it's hardly ever completely exclusive of one another. At the other end of the spectrum, one may draw the line too easily. As if a pill is all you need. I can tell you this: at best, pills can help you manage depression, they can help you learn to live with it, they can lift the most paralyzing black blanket and enable you to get back some control, to live your life in a way so you are no longer a victim of your illness. But they're not a cure. They can't make you happy. Happiness is still very much our responsibility and has nothing to do with the disease. Just as it is our responsibility to deal and address conflict that arises, face necessary struggles, and respect and accommodate love and relationships. Happiness is no guar-antee and can't be medically induced. The ability to live your life fully is, however, something one can be robbed of by the disease. And all this is just the tip of the iceberg. Depression is long, tedious, hard work, and once you get through the thick of it and are lucky enough to survive it, the real work begins (like it does at the end of the movie). Even under the best of circumstances, when you have people who love you and who try to understand and accept you for who you are, living with this illness is hard.

W&H: The film premiered over a year ago at Sundance. Why did it
        take so long for it to come to theaters?

SN: More often than not, it is frustrating, demoralizing, and some-
        times infuriating how little control one has over this aspect of
        the filmmaking process. Not to say that there has ever been an
        easy time to release a challenging film, but the last couple of
        years certainly haven't been favorable for independent drama.
        I have to say I am very happy that the film will see the light of
        day at all in the United States. I feel that that is where this film
        really belongs. I surely wish it had received a lot more exposure
        than it has.

W&H: **What are you working on next?**

SN: I'm adapting a French novella about an American widower in
        Paris. It's a charming, bittersweet, and melancholic comedy. It
        reminds me in many ways of *Mostly Martha* and, once again,
        revolves around the themes that you can find in each one of the
        five films I've made so far—who is part of the family, what we
        do for love, and what love can do for us.

Pratibha Parmar
FILM TITLE: *Nina's Heavenly Delights*

Date of Release (or festival premiere): 2006 Bite the Mango Film Festival (UK)

Link to IMDb Page: www.imdb.com/title/tt0435706

Link to Site: www.ninasheavenlydelights.com

Link to Trailer: www.ninasheavenlydelights.com/video.html

BIO: British filmmaker Pratibha Parmar has spent more than twenty years behind the camera bringing fresh perspectives to stories of women, minorities, and social issues. Her award-winning work has been exhibited widely at international film festivals and broadcast in many countries. *Nina's Heavenly Delights*, her feature film debut, was released in the United Kingdom and the United States in 2006/2007. Born in Kenya, of Indian decent, Parmar moved with her family to England at a young age. Following university in England, she began her filmmaking career with documentary shorts as a way to express her passion in representations of subjects and issues not in the mainstream.

In 1991, her career reached a critical turning point with the release of *A Place of Rage*, a documentary about African American women's role in the Civil Rights Movement. In 1993, Parmar released *Warrior Marks*, which documented ritual female mutilation in Africa, which came at a time when the subject was still taboo in the international community. Parmar has directed music videos and is the co-author and editor of several books. She is a past winner of the San Francisco Frameline Film Festival Lifetime Achievement Award. (Credit: Kai Films)

DESCRIPTION: *Nina's Heavenly Delights* is a surprising love story where Scottish humor meets Bollywood spectacle! It follows the mixed fortunes of a Glaswegian family, the Shahs, and their award-winning Indian restaurant, The New Taj.

The story is told through the eyes of Nina Shah, a young Scottish Asian woman. Nina had left home under a cloud after an argument with her father, but when he dies suddenly, Nina is forced to return. Her return reunites her with her childhood friend Bobbi, a wannabe Bollywood drag queen, and brings her face to face with Lisa, a charismatic young woman who now owns half the restaurant.

Then Nina discovers her father's secret—The New Taj has been selected for The Best of the West Curry Competition. In the turbulent, but exhilarating days that follow, Nina, with Lisa's help, embarks on a personal mission to win the trophy for the third time. But Nina's feelings are thrown into turmoil when she realizes that she is falling in love. (Credit: *Nina's Heavenly Delights* Official Website)

Interview Date: November 19, 2007

WOMEN AND HOLLYWOOD: **Why was it important for you to tell this story?**

PRATIBHA PARMAR: Many reasons. One of the common wisdoms in the film industry is that you should always make your first film about something personal. So I chose to write a story that was based on my own experience of falling in love in a way and with a person that was a complete surprise! I wanted to tell a story that had at its heart a nontraditional, 'forbidden love' but using a traditional genre like romantic comedy.

W&H: **It took seven years from writing the story until production. How did you persevere in your vision throughout that time?**

PP: Now I know why they say make your first film about some-
        thing you feel passionate about—because in that long seven-
        year-journey to get this film onto the screen, it really was
        sheer blind passion and determination that helped me to keep
        going. You hear so many more no's then you ever hear maybe
        or yes. It was also pride and sometimes anger that kept me
        going. I could see male directors with half the experience that
        I have making their debut features without the kind of intense
        struggle that I was going through, without having to "prove"
        that they were ready to make a feature.

        By the time I had come to make *Nina's Heavenly Delights*, I had
        already made award-winning documentaries and also directed
        a number of short dramas. So it was frustrating to say the least
        when potential financiers kept asking me if I was confident
        enough to direct drama and if I could work with a big crew. I
        don't think the majority of men in the film industry interna-
        tionally have an innate sense of confidence in women directors
        in the way they do with male directors.

W&H: **Did you write the film knowing that you would direct it?
        Do you think that more women directors are writing their
        own scripts because so few scripts are available to them to
        direct?**

PP: Oh yes, when I wrote the story, it was very much with a view
        to directing it. I am a director first and foremost and want to
        tell stories that I don't often see on the cinema screens. I think
        first we have to be *seen* as directors to be even sent scripts for
        consideration. I always have to generate my own work and that
        can often mean that you have to wait so many more years until
        you make your next feature. So it would be lovely to be sent
        scripts that have already gone through "development hell" and
        are ready to go into production.

W&H: **Music is a very important element in the film and brings life
to many of the scenes, especially Bobbi's. Talk a little about
the importance of music in telling this story.**

PP: Music has always been a key storytelling device for me. I had
chosen some of the songs in the film very early on. I wanted
the texture of the music to reflect the world of the film, which
is a cross-cultural and cross-everything else kind of world.
The few Bollywood songs in the film have lyrics that help
to advance the narrative. And then there are also contemporary pop songs like The Monkees' "Day Dream Believer"
and tracks from some great female singer/songwriters like
Alex Parkes, Shelley Poole, and Holly Vallance, whom many
people will recognize. Music can trigger so many different
emotional responses, and you don't always need dialogue
when a lyric or a musical refrain can evoke the mood or story
so much more effectively.

W&H: **What do you want people to get out of this film?**

PP: I want people to leave the cinema feeling happy, hungry, and
horny. No seriously—I want people to see the characters
beyond their sexuality or culture. The film showed on British
Airways long-haul flights last Christmas and a friend was
traveling from London to Delhi when it was screening. He got
his whole cabin to watch the movie and at first a few of the
Indian mothers were saying, "Oh dear, we didn't know this
happened in our communities"—i.e., a woman falling in love
with another woman—but then halfway through the film, he
said everyone forgot that Nina is gay and were rooting for her
to win the cooking competition. It was great to hear that.

W&H: **There are so few films released in the United States that feature female leads, and you not only have a woman lead, she is
Asian and realizing she is gay. How is the film being marketed**

so that the widest audience possible will be exposed to the story? Do you think that the audience will be gay people, Asian people, Scottish people, women, or all of the above?

PP: I hope that the audience will be people of every color, sexuality, and musical tastes. Everyone who enjoys a feel-good movie! So far the film has screened at more than fifty international film festivals—many of them mainstream festivals and some for niche markets. But across the board, the audiences have loved it. From Hong Kong to India to Paris to Turin, people have responded very positively.

The U.S. distributors, Regent Releasing, have been fantastic so far. They totally get that the movie has great potential to break out into the mainstream and so they are trying (with their limited resources) to get the word out there. Ultimately with films that are not "star" led or have some kind of celebrity marketing push, it's the *word of mouth* that is crucial. So I really hope people who have seen it and like it blog about it, get onto Rotten Tomatoes and other sites and write or vote for it and help spread a buzz.

W&H: What does it mean to be a woman director in a world where so few women are directors? Do you feel an added responsibility?

PP: The main responsibility I feel is to myself as a storyteller and to make films with truthfulness, honesty, and integrity. In doing so, if the work inspires other women to want to become direc-tors, then that's terrific, but I am not into carrying that burden of responsibility for all women or all minorities for that matter. Having said that, I am an Associate of the Birds Eye View Women's Film Festival in the United Kingdom, and have been their supporter since they first formed. As an active member of Women in Film & Television in the United Kingdom, I helped to initiate the Women Directing Change program where less experienced women directors get the opportunity to shadow more experienced film directors, both men and women. The abysmally low number of women directors is appalling—so I am supportive of anything that helps to change that.

Photo credit: Sally Potter

Sally Potter

FILM TITLE: *Rage*

Date of Release (or festival premiere): September 2009 (Babelgum.com), mobile download.

Link to IMDb page: www.imdb.com/title/tt1234550

Link to Site: ragethemovie.com

Link to Trailer: ragethemovie.com/trailer

BIO: Sally Potter has had an eclectic career that has included dance, theatre, music, and film. In 1983 she directed her first feature, *The Gold Diggers*, starring Julie Christie. She received internationally acclaim for the multi-award winning film *Orlando*, starring Tilda Swinton. Potter also directed *Carmen* for English National Opera in Autumn 2007. Potter's film, *Rage*, starring Judi Dench, Jude Law, Steve Buscemi, Simon Abkarian, and Dianne Wiest was released in 2009. Her most recent film is Ginger and Rosa.

DESCRIPTION: Sally Potter is a filmmaking icon. She is an outspoken, visionary, feminist director who has been on the cutting edge of the indie world since she started making films. Potter's work is an acquired taste, and her new film, *Rage,* once again pushes all the boundaries in form and in the method of distribution. The movie stars high-profile people (Jude Law, Judi Dench, among others) in a series of intimate interviews at a fashion show. As the film progresses, you get to know more and more about what makes these people who they are.

Interview Date: September 29, 2009

WOMEN & HOLLYWOOD: To me, *Rage* is such an intimate movie. First, do you think it's intimate, and second, where did you get your inspiration from?

SALLY POTTER: I do think it is intimate. It is a word I use a lot. It is in part my direct experience from being on the Internet and doing a blog and making myself accessible to people in a very intimate way and finding that for the first time in all my working life, I was having a one-on-one global relationship with strangers who I would otherwise never meet, who in my imagination I was working for. So, as I began to understand the nature of the Internet with this peculiar combination of global reach and intimate relationships, it gave me a clue about how to make a different kind of film, one that would incorporate some of this language of the Internet.

W&H: **So I guess we can call this one of the first web 2.0 inspired movies?**

SP: Certainly, and of course, the first film ever released on a cell phone.

W&H: **There seems to be such a crisis in independent filmmaking with people really freaked out about the future.**

SP: It's not just the independents; it's the studios, too.

W&H: **How are you going to monetize this film if people can download it for free on their cell phone?**

SP: First of all, I've always had an evolutionary approach to survival as a filmmaker. Indeed, like the principle of evolution, those who adapt survive, those who don't become dinosaurs. So, I figure that in this age of the terror of theft on the Internet, the cleverest thing to do is give it away. When you remove that terror you free your imagination to start to think about how to get your money back in more imaginative ways. There seems to be some early experience and statistics to suggest that downloads in music, for example, do not stop people from buying CDs, but it builds awareness and creates a larger audience, which will, in turn, stimulate more people to buy, paradoxically. Similarly, there is even the beginning of statistics showing that (film) piracy stimulates a larger audience, which, in turn, stimulates more buying. So that means income through DVDs. In the case of our film, we sold it—albeit not for a massive sum—to Babelgum, who are putting it out, so there is some cash flowing back from the beginning. This is an extremely low budget film—which was deliberately kept low. I call it barefoot filmmaking. It's a way of filmmaking for survival.

W&H: **The word *rage* is such a loaded word, and I wanted to get a sense of why you picked that for the title.**

SP: There is an element of punning in it—about "all the rage," a phrase that is hardly used anymore. But I think there is a deeper feeling of rage, a kind of quiet rage on a mass scale, and not knowing where to focus this rage, which is the negative end of globalization. The positive end is the Internet, in my view, but the negative end is about greater and greater ownership by anonymous corporate entities and less and less about freedom for the individual. Now, of course, what has happened—the banking crisis has brought a lot to the fore, and now people do have a target for their anger, against an amoral profiteering system, against a genuinely, purely amoral *money-in-the-pocket* and *who-cares-about-anybody-else* way of thinking. And I think that the fashion industry, like every other industry, links into that globalized anonymous ownership—and that end of it is a bit nasty, so the rage could be the rage of the outworkers who are underpaid, it could be the stereotyping of beauty that leads to this terrible mass anorexia that so many young women suffer from, and all the other ways that world interfaces with the big difficult thing that most people don't have a language for.

W&H: **So the rage is a microcosm of all the crazy different things we go through every day.**

SP: Yes, at some level we are in a rage and don't even know it.

W&H: **On your blog you used the term *poor cinema* to describe this film. Can you explain the concept?**

SP: I mean it in the sense of (Jerzy) Grotowski in theater and other people who are taking the element of their form back to the basic. Poor in the sense of minimal or austere—no waste, direct, simple in its means, simple in its execution. There are certain things that don't cost money but take energy and time, so although *YouTube* and very cheap cameras make it possible for anyone to do a film, it doesn't make it possible for them to make them well.

W&H: **So how do you live, how do you pay your rent or mortgage? The first thing they tell you about making a movie is don't invest your own money.**

SP: Well, I like breaking all the rules, and that's why I am putting this movie out there for free when everyone else is terrified of precisely that. I've never not gone into debt when I first starting out making a movie. I've gotten used to it and I've learned how to surf it, if you like, and eventually the money comes back because everything I have made has actually sold. So the income does come back eventually, it's just that I have, in effect, to become an investor in my own work at the beginning. So that's how I think of the debt, as an investment in myself. I got started by saying, "If nobody else wants to back me, I'm going to back myself." I'm not wealthy; I don't come from a wealthy family. But that's the way I'm going to get this work made. I'm going to be prepared to work harder than anyone else.

W&H: **Do you think that women have to work harder to get their vision out there?**

SP: Quite possibly, but all the male filmmakers I know are also struggling, I must say that. However, we are still in this insane minority.

W&H: **You write that for you filmmaking is a poetic, personal, and political necessity. Most people don't think about making movies in that way. What is it about movies that makes you need to do them?**

SP: That really is the million dollar question, *the why*. I know how
to recognize the sensation. When I am searching in my own
mind for the next film to do, I'm looking for that sensation
which is—*I must do*. I absolutely *have to* do this, rather than,
it *might sell* or what do *other people* want me to do or those
other considerations. The impulse has to come from deep
within and an absolute commitment. And passion—because
it takes so bloody long and you have to sustain difficulties and
downtime. But I think the feeling of poetic, political, and personal necessity, which is a marriage of three different kinds of
sensibilities, is probably a sort of triad of motivations that any
artist would have in common, whether a painter or poet and,
possibly, a scientist and mathematician. It's somebody who
thinks with a sense of purpose through producing something
for others.

W&H: **What are you thinking about doing next?**

SP: Until I've put one thing to bed—or out into the world—I'm
not really free to put all my attention into finding the next
project. The interactive premiere we had last night (September
24, 2009) here in the United Kingdom was the last of this,
and in a week or two, I will be free to work fully on the next
thing. But I also want to learn from this process. How does it
actually work? Are people going to buy the DVD or not? Are
they going to be watching it on their cell phone? How is word
going to spread? How does viral word-of-mouth work in this
modern cutting edge of film? Is this a kind of film that people
are going to like and enjoy, with this level of simplicity?

In my own life, I tend to have a kind of pendulum—a smaller
film, a bigger film, a smaller film, a bigger film, so it might be
that I want to do a bigger film next. And I do know, and I've
learned this cumulatively, that people really, really, really, want

to connect with something that matters—it can be a comedy or tragedy, it doesn't matter—but they want to connect from the heart with the material.

W&H: **There are not a lot of women who talk about their politics and feminism in their work and it is still such a struggle for women to get their film made. Any thoughts?**

SP: It is making some headway because, when I first started, there were no women in the context where I was working. And that was a very lonely place, and I've watched that shift gradually. People used to come to me in all parts of the world and said, "Oh, I loved *The Piano,*" and I said, "No, that was Jane [Campion]." And she and I would meet up now and then at festivals and she would say that people keep telling her they love *Orlando.* So, it was as if there were two of us in a sort of vaguely conspicuous, visible place in the pantheon of directors and that's changed surely. So that's already an advance.

But I think I am in a slightly different category than most women, because I am not waiting to be offered work. I do get offered scripts but so far I've turned them all down. I write my own, so I don't go in the waiting position. I generate my own material. I initiate it, I set it up, I retain control—and that, if anything, is my secret on how to proceed because there is nothing diluted.

W&H: **Lots of women are writers and directors because that is some-times the only chance they get to direct.**

SP: Yes. That means putting in a lot of hours into the writing pro-cess—I mean, years—because, of course, it's not the same thing as directing. They are a different activity all together. There's a downside to it and there's an upside too, which is you become the complete author of your work.

W&H: **Do you have advice for young women who want to become filmmakers?**

SP: Yes. Don't give up. And get started. It takes longer if you don't get started.

Photo Credit: David Cole

Cathy Randall

FILM TITLE: *Hey Hey It's Esther Blueberger*

Date of Release (or festival premiere): 2008 Berlin International Film Festival

Link to IMDb Page: www.imdb.com/title/tt0469099

Link to Site: www.montereymedia.com/theatrical/films/blueburger.html

Link to Trailer: www.montereymedia.com/independent/hey_hey_trailer.html

---

BIO: Cathy Randall started her career as a writer for the Australian soap opera *Home and Away*. She interned at Scott Free Productions in Los Angeles before being awarded a scholarship to the Los Angeles Film School's Feature Development Program in 2002. It was through this program that Randall developed the *Hey Hey It's Esther Blueberger* screenplay. Randall is currently co-writing the screenplay for *Nim's Island 2*.

113

DESCRIPTION: *Hey Hey It's Esther Blueberger* is about a thirteen-year-old Australian girl who has trouble fitting in with all the girls at school as she prepares for her Bat Mitzvah. Esther is played by newcomer Danielle Catanzariti, and, to me, she is the perfect tween heroine—a girl awkwardly trying to negotiate adolescence while refusing to buy into typical girl culture. Stuck in a private school where no one talks to her, Esther then meets Sunni (Keisha Castle-Hughes), and she devises a story that gets her into public school (without her parents knowing). In public school (acting like a Swedish exchange student), Esther finds a tribe where she can fit in and be popular in her own way.

This is a film for any kid (and adult) who has struggled to fit in.

Interview Date: April 29, 2010

WOMEN AND HOLLYWOOD: This was your first film and you got a top tier cast. How did that happen?

CATHY RANDALL: It was actually very straightforward. After seeing *Whale Rider*, I felt Keisha Castle-Hughes would make a wonderful Sunni, so we sent her the script while the film was still in development. She read it very quickly and got back to me within days with an extremely positive response. She really identified with the script and the character and immediately wanted to do the film. It took another three years before we went into production, and we were really worried Keisha would get too old to play a thirteen-year-old. She was sixteen when we shot the film; but because Sunni (the character she plays) has grown up too quickly and is so full of wisdom it ended up working for her. Toni Collette was a natural choice for Mary. Besides being an exceptional actress, she exudes such warmth and vitality onscreen that I knew she would capture Mary perfectly. As with Keisha, it was very straightforward. We sent the script to her agent and she liked it and agreed to do the film. Both Keisha and Toni really reacted to the script above all else.

W&H: **You wrote the script for the film in 2002 and it took until 2007 for the film to go into production. Why do you think it took so long?**

CR: I wrote the first draft of the script in 2002 but it really was a first draft. It took me another couple of years to perfect it. When I met Miriam Stein, the film's producer, I did another rewrite and we started pitching it to potential financiers. It took a couple of years to raise the financing and then we had to wait several more months to fit in with Toni's schedule before we could go into production.

W&H: **Where did you get the idea for the story?**

CR: It was very loosely based on personal experience. For me, thirteen was such an intense time of growth, change, and self-discovery and I really wanted to explore this—the grey zone between childhood and adulthood—in a fresh way and from a female point of view.

W&H: **There are so few coming-of-age stories for girls. This film is so rare in that it is real but also plays up Esther's true nature. Why do you think there are so few stories about girls, especially ones where they aren't hypersexualized?**

CR: I really wish I knew. It was a constant source of frustration for me growing up (and still is). And that is why I was so determined to make this film. There are so few films with female protagonists—full stop. I think in the past this has largely been due to the perception that films with female protagonists don't sell. But I'm optimistic. This is changing, especially with the recent success of *Sex and the City* and *Mamma Mia!*

W&H: What is different about making films in Australia vs. the United States?

CR: It's hard for me to say, having never made a film in the United States, but I think making films in Australia would be much like making indie films in the United States. Budgets are lower but you have more creative control over the end product.

W&H: Do you feel you are a writer or a director first? And now that you have directed your own material, do you see yourself continuing in that manner?

CR: I really enjoy doing both. When I made *Hey Hey It's Esther Blueburger* I felt that the directing was an extension of the writing. I wrote the script in order to direct it, so it really felt like it was part and parcel of the same storytelling process. I would love to continue directing my own material but I don't feel the need to do this exclusively. I would also love to direct someone else's script if I felt a connection to it.

W&H: What's next for you?

CR: I'm currently writing the sequel to *Nim's Island* for Walden Media in the States. I'm also working with a wonderful writer called Melina Marchetta, adapting one of her novels—*Jellicoe Road*—for the screen (Melina is writing, and I'll be directing). And I'm writing a couple of other scripts, which I hope to direct.

W&H: What advice do you have for other female writers and directors?

CR: Only to keep working, to keep telling stories. I think the more female filmmakers we have, the more our screens will open up to female protagonists and three-dimensional female characters. We still have such a long way to go with this and it would be great to see it change.

Amy Redford

Date of Release (or festival premiere): 2008 Sundance Film Festival

Link to IMDb Page: www.imdb.com/title/tt0942891

Link to Trailer: www.youtube.com/watch?v=Jhm2LsnJz8I

BIO: Amy Redford made her directorial debut with *The Guitar*, which premiered at the 2008 Sundance Film Festival. She has a degree in drama/theater from San Francisco State University. As an actress, she has appeared in numerous TV shows and movies, including *Sex and the City* and *Sunshine Cleaning*. Current directing projects include *El Americano* and *Phoenix*.

DESCRIPTION: *The Guitar* is a tour de force for English actress Saffron Burrows. She plays Melody Wilder, an unhappy woman who is invisible to most around her and is given a month to live with advanced cancer of the larynx. She abandons her life as she knew it, rents a loft, and prepares for her demise by running up her credit cards and learning to play the guitar she had been dreaming about her whole life. Turns out that in changing everything about herself and her life, she tricked her cancer into a full remission. Melody now has to deal with the consequences of her spending, as well as the new life she has created for herself, full of creativity and on her own terms.

The film is a true character study. Burrows is alone for most of the film. She begins the film literally—and figuratively—with no voice and at the conclusion she is reborn and finds her true, authentic voice.

Interview Date: November 7, 2008

WOMEN AND HOLLYWOOD: **In the beginning, people just talk at Melody and the words seem to bounce off her. When she's alone and sick she finds her voice. It struck me that she found her voice with barely any words.**

AMY REDFORD: I went through a period in my life in my twenties when I had chronic laryngitis for three years, and I realize now that I was not my authentic self. I was shut off so I totally related to the condition of the character. There is a quality of the physical manifestation that I thought was fascinating. Or the fact that the character is left to be on her own, even without the devices she brings in to the room—that's the scariest. She goes through this journey of buying the things, but ultimately it's an appetite that will never be sated because what it's really about is not what you buy, it's really about the quiet. So that moment when she found her voice, it is like a rebirth—powerful and joyous.

W&H: **How did you get the script?**

AR: I was introduced to Amos Poe (the screenwriter) by a friend who thought I would be right for the lead role. I heard the story that inspired the script and I was haunted by the premise. I kept firing myself from the part and hiring other actors in my head. I had been looking for a project to direct for a while, and I knew this was the one when the images started coming to me naturally.

W&H: **Do you still want to act?**

AR: My passion lies in directing, but I don't want to quit acting completely because it's important to stay flexible. It's easy to be dismissive about actors because sometimes they are high maintenance. But being able to use all my faculties is really satisfying, so directing feels like an evolution for me.

W&H: **Lots of women directors also write their own stories. Are you a writer?**

AR: I really love the collaborative process and working with writers. I think now there is a bigger window for stories about women than there has been. The blank page is daunting to me.

W&H: **What's the message of this film?**

AR: It's funny; I should be so good at answering this question. What you take away from it is such a personal experience. It's really about questioning whether you are using the currency of your life to the fullest capacity. That's different for everybody and what they would do in the face of mortality is different for everybody. This movie isn't meant to be a prescription; it's meant to be a conversation. It can be literal when you are facing an illness, or metaphorical when you hit a roadblock, or a turning point in your life. I hope people make their own conclusions. I don't want to tell someone what to feel.

W&H: **Do you think that women have a hard time finding their voice?**

AR: I think it's easier for women to submerge their voice. I think that women innately have wonderful things to say, but in order to accommodate others, it's easier for us to put our own voice aside. Even the loudest women are loud for a reason—because they can't be heard. I just had a daughter two months ago, and I hope that whatever I do has a positive influence on her chances of not having to fight so hard. This election (the 2008 presidential election of Barack Obama) has shown us a lot of different ways to be a woman. Like her or not, Sarah Palin made it to the table and there is something to be said for that. It is interesting how the conversation was not about the fact that she was a woman but about what kind of woman she was. On the other hand, we have Hillary Clinton who is beloved by so many. It's an interesting time and the conversation is steering more toward substance.

W&H: **This film was a real departure for Saffron Burrows. Were you nervous about having to make her look not as beautiful as she really is?**

AR: I think it speaks to her emotional sophistication. I learned a lot because I felt she was too beautiful and was worried that people were going to be alienated by her beauty. But then I realized I was perpetuating the same thing and I had to give myself a spanking. It was the realization that it's really about the light that you have inside and what you project. You can be a beautiful person but if you are shut down inside you are not going to attract people, and you can be unconventional looking and be projecting a kind of life force that people can't get enough of. She so completely understood what I meant that I knew she was right for the part. She was at the perfect moment in her life and her career. She had a lack of vanity that allowed her to be truthful, which I appreciated. We shot the film chronologically so my job was to start her off in the right place, to begin the film in the right pitch, and then go for the ride and see what happens.

W&H: **Was it a small budget?**

AR: The shoot was twenty-one days long and the budget was really small. I can't even talk about it, but as it goes in the independent film business, one second you have the money and the next the union guys are knocking on your door and you come to work and people are like, "Hello, where's my paycheck?" which is horrifying. But, at the same time, people are generous.

W&H: **This movie is really coming in under the radar screen with very little publicity. Is that frustrating?**

AR: It can be frustrating, but one of the things that makes it worthwhile is the amount of letters I have received from people—people struggling with cancer and people who had their own emotional rebirth. People are hungry for these kinds of things. I can't control the other stuff. I just need to stay focused on what my job is. I learned a lot about film finance on this movie, and I implore people, especially women filmmakers, to really go to school on budgets and money because that's the protection around the creative element. You empower yourself. It's like the big lesson for women everywhere—money is your freedom.

Patricia Riggen

FILM TITLE: *La Misma Luna*

Date of Release (or festival premiere): March 19, 2008

Link to IMDb Page: www.imdb.com/title/tt0796307

Link to Site: www.foxsearchlight.com/underthesamemoon

Link to Trailer: www.foxsearchlight.com/underthesamemoon

BIO: Patricia Riggen is a Mexican film director. She is best known for directing *La Misma Luna/Under the Same Moon* and the 2011 Disney Channel original film *Lemonade Mouth*.

Riggen was born in Guadalajara, where she gained experience in journalism and writing for documentaries. She later moved to New York City, where she received her master's degree in directing and screenwriting from Columbia University. In 2008, *La Misma Luna*, Riggen's first major film was released, starring America Ferrera. She also has directed *Revolución*, starring Eva Mendes. Her film, *Girl in Progress*, starring Eva Mendes, was released in 2012. She is currently working on the film *Elsa and Fred*.

DESCRIPTION: *La Misma Luna* was, suffice to say, an unexpected pleasure. While I do like my share of foreign films, I sometimes walk into them expecting something overly serious and sometimes difficult to relate to. This film was nothing like that. *La Misma Luna* (*Under the Same Moon*) is a beautiful and touching film that tells the incredibly relevant story of a mother and son separated by the U.S. border, each trying to survive the best they can without one another.

Rosario (Kate Del Castillo) has crossed the U.S. border from Mexico in order to provide for her son, Carlitos (Adrian Alonso), whom she left with her mother. Rosario tells him that when he misses her he should look up at the moon because they would both be looking at the same moon and would feel closer together. When Carlitos' grandmother dies unexpectedly, the nine-year-old sets off on the perilous journey to find his mother just as she is struggling with the decision about whether to return to Mexico to be with him. Riggen takes the hot political issue of immigration and humanizes it in a profound way. It never gets preachy, is extremely moving, and has an amazingly breathtaking performance from a talented young actor, Adrian Alonso.

Interview Date: March 19, 2008

WOMEN AND HOLLYWOOD: The issue of immigration is so highly
    charged, and you were able to humanize it and also to show
    that it is a women's issue.

PATRICIA RIGGEN: Women are now crossing the border. It used to be
    men. Now, there are four million women in this country who
    have left a child behind. When people ask me if this is a true
    story, I tell them that it is based on four million true stories.
    These women have no other option and make the most difficult
    sacrifice of all, because no mother would leave her child unless
    she was desperate. That was something I wanted to explore.
    Rosario has a huge dilemma. Having made this decision in
    order to provide for her child because she loves him, at the
    same time, she feels like she is sacrificing that love. It's not just
    a statistic to me. These are human beings and that's what I
    wanted to show.

W&H: This film feels very female—it's from a woman's eye. It's no
    coincidence that both the director and screenwriter are women.
    These films are few and far between in Hollywood these days.

PR: It's something that I have struggled with in my career. I'm
    Mexican, and I could never have become a director in Mexico.
    I moved here and that allowed me to do this work.

W&H: In Mexico you didn't have an opportunity to work as a
    director?

PR: In Mexico, I never gave myself the chance to imagine myself
    in the director's shoes. It took me a while to discover what I
    wanted to do. I was already working in the business doing
    different jobs and feeling unhappy. When I was growing up in
    Mexico, there weren't any women directors around for me to
    see that it was something I could do. Funny enough, I wrote

my college thesis on women directors in Mexico when I didn't even know I was going to be a director. There were four, and I interviewed them feeling like being a director was equivalent to being an astronaut—the hardest, strangest thing to be—completely inaccessible and it shouldn't be like that.

W&H: **Women feel that it is so difficult to be a director here.**

PR: That's what my friends tell me and I feel it is so easy here.

W&H: **Have the Fox Searchlight people (the film's distributor) been supporting your vision?**

PR: Fox Searchlight has been wonderful and I'll tell you why—they're all women. There's one guy at the top and then it's all women. Their sensibility is very feminine and it makes it really wonderful for a women's movie. They totally get it and care about the film.

W&H: **Adrian Alonso's performance as Carlitos really astounded me. Talk a little bit about how you directed him and how you were able to elicit his spectacular performance.**

PR: Thank you, nobody ever asks me about this. They always say, where did you find him. It's not the finding; it's the directing. It's all about the directing. I think most kids can act and it's a matter of directing them properly. In this case, Adrian is very talented but he's also a child and has no criteria to understand if he is doing something good or not. Older actors know what they are doing, kids don't.

W&H: **The whole movie rests on his shoulders.**

PR: I basically knew that if I didn't find the right kid I shouldn't even attempt to make this movie. But the truth is that I worked with him very closely and my eyes were always on him to protect and help him.

W&H: **How did you get the script?**

PR: I made a documentary called *Family Portraits,* and Ligiah
          Villalobos (the writer) saw it and loved it and sent me the
          screenplay. I immediately connected with it. We started
          working together, and when we had the script ready to shoot
          the financing was there. She was great to work with, she's very
          smart and she always stood by me. When I felt that the movie
          wasn't going to happen, she came and worked for no money.
          She did all the drafts and revisions and waited and waited for
          the movie to happen.

W&H: **You are also the film's producer.**

PR: This is an important aspect. I did have a way to make this at
          a studio and I started working with them but felt I was losing
          creative control and the decisions being made were wrong and
          it wasn't going to be a good movie. I was thinking that I was a
          director for hire, but it was a project that I brought and realized
          this is not a way I wanted to make my first feature. Fortunately,
          it was a very low budget so I decided to raise the money myself
          to keep control and to make every single decision, which
          allowed me to make the best movie I could.

W&H: **What do you want the audience to feel after seeing the film?**

PR: I want them to have a good time, and to feel engaged and
          moved. I want people to see the humanity of those who sur-
          round us that we don't necessarily notice—like the waiter or
          the gardener—and think about their lives.

W&H: **What's next for you?**

PR: I have several offers from Hollywood. I am keeping my feet
          on the ground knowing that my fellow female directors have
          taken a long time to shoot again. They have made successful
          first films and then it has taken them a long time to shoot

their second. I don't want to take ten years to make another film. I am developing some projects for Hollywood, including a romantic comedy and a period drama. But I also have a project of my own that I control in case the Hollywood films don't happen.

Photo Credit: The World Unseen Films, Ltd.

Shamim Sarif

FILM TITLE: *The World Unseen*

Date of Release (or festival premiere): November 2008

Link to IMDb page: www.imdb.com/title/tt1048174

Link to Trailer: http://youtu.be/jlD3EprZp5M

FILM TITLE: *I Can't Think Straight*

Date of Release (or festival premiere): November 2008

Link to IMDb page: www.imdb.com/title/tt0830570

Link to Trailer: http://youtu.be/1W8igqK_QWU

BIO: Writer/director Shamim Sarif is an amazingly versatile artist. She is a successful author; her first novel won several awards. She is the author of several published short stories, music lyrics, a children's TV series, and screenplays. She also directed music videos feature films. Shamim has deep roots in South Africa, where her parents and grandparents were born and raised—a heritage that inspired her first, award-winning novel, *The World Unseen*. She finished her third film—a documentary, *The House of Tomorrow*—in 2011.

DESCRIPTION: *The World Unseen* tells a very different story of 1950s Apartheid South Africa. It's the story of two Indian women: one, Amina, living an unconventional life as a cafe owner with a black business partner, and another, Miriam, a very traditional woman trapped in a difficult marriage. Amina is independent, wears pants, and bucks conventions. Miriam takes care of her husband and children, but is miserable. Amina shows Miriam the possibilities of independence and personal freedom and gives her the tools to change her life, which unexpectedly leads to romance.

I Can't Think Straight is a story of two young women in London: Tala, a spirited Jordanian who comes from a Christian family and is about to marry her fiancé, and Leyla, a quiet, British Indian with a strong Muslim upbringing. Despite their differences, these two girls are immediately attracted to one another. They eventually share their feelings, but Tala cannot bring herself to break off her engagement and flies to Jordan to complete wedding preparations. It isn't until the wedding day approaches that Tala recognizes the value of being true to oneself and sets off to reconcile—and win back—the woman she loves.

Interview Date: November 7, 2008

WOMEN AND HOLLYWOOD: Two films, the same actresses, dealing with lesbian issues opening within two weeks of each other. Are you crazy?

SHAMIM SARIF: There was no long-term reasoning behind this release pattern. It wasn't about a woman's story or a lesbian story or anything like that because at the time we made the movies, I wasn't looking at it from a distribution point of view. I was passionate about making strong stories and these two screenplays got financed. To be honest, my partner and I and the executive producers and the lead actresses never looked at it as "Oh, we're doing another lesbian film." They looked at each one in terms of story and characters—they are very different genres—one is a period piece and the other is a romantic comedy. When we completed both around the same time, our North American distributor thought that a close release would enable them to capitalize on publicity and give the release an unusual spin. But it wasn't a forced situation of holding one film back—they were both ready around the same time.

W&H: **Which did you make first?**

SS: We shot *I Can't Think Straight* first and it got stuck in limbo when the financing collapsed soon after the shoot finished (or mostly finished!). Then my partner and producer Hanan managed to get *The World Unseen* going, which was a blessing after the pain of losing *I Can't Think Straight*. By the time we got back *I Can't Think Straight*, both movies were in post-production at the same time.

W&H: **What do you mean by "got it back"?**

SS: We had a first investor, a guy who turned out to be a crook and we found out he hadn't been paying bills. He had the film negative and we had the story rights because he never paid me. It took us more than a year to fight him in court. It was hard and expensive and I was tempted to walk away as it seemed a high mountain to climb. But Hanan was incredibly tenacious and in the meantime we made *The World Unseen*. We literally finished them both about a month ago.

W&H: **How did you not know the bills weren't being taken care of?**

SS: The actors were paid so we didn't know what was happening until afterward. An amazing amount in film production (and in business generally) gets done on faith—you rent a location, they send you an invoice, they don't expect payment for thirty days. The movie took twenty-five days to shoot. Then you're sitting in a nightmare.

The happy story about this is that *The World Unseen* was a much better financed film—purely by female financiers. They are not gay women—they are savvy businesswomen who just loved the book and wanted to see that vision onscreen. One of the investors crossed over to *I Can't Think Straight* and we got another one to come in and then I was able to finish the movie.

W&H: **How much were the budgets?**

SS: Under $3 million for *The World Unseen* and less than $1 million for *I Can't Think Straight*.

W&H: **Did you write both scripts?**

SS: Yes, I did. *The World Unseen* was adapted from my novel of the same name, and it felt like a natural progression because I had written a screenplay before (adapted from a short story I published). I think the book is quite visual, and that helped translate it to the screen, but I love what David Hare says, which is that you have to be promiscuous to be faithful in adaptation. *I Can't Think Straight* started as a novel and I got a little bogged down in the structure, so Hanan (cleverly!) suggested I write it as a script first. But I wanted it to be lighter than the novel so I worked with a good friend Kelly Moss who has a fantastic sense of humor. She really helped with the funnier parts of the movie.

W&H: **Is it based on your life?**

SS: It's slightly autobiographical in terms of the cultures and certain events. But quite heavily dramatized, as well. For instance, Hanan was not engaged when I met her, but that made a more compelling film storyline. Although it's specific to Palestinian and Indian cultures, the challenges and emotions the women and their families face are quite universal.

W&H: **Hollywood doesn't think that women's stories are universal. We are still seen as the other, as a niche. What was your experience with that?**

SS: It didn't occur to me that it wouldn't be financially viable to write a woman's story. It's just what came to me, these strong characters. For *The World Unseen,* I wanted to write about integrity and about finding your voice, which is something women traditionally need to do especially at the time and place of the movie. For me, the whole journey of the movie was Miriam finding her independence and her voice; and the person who helps her do that is someone who has already found her voice. I had a strong vision for the novel and having strong material to start with was crucial because people will respond, or not, to the quality of the story. In the indie world the quality of the story is paramount. But yes, financing on a large scale is just not as available, but I have to follow my passion and continue to write strong female leads because we still have some way to go in believing that women's stories are as compelling. And there is no reason for that not to be the case.

W&H: **How did you wind up with the same actresses starring in both films?**

SS: I knew I wanted to work with Lisa (Ray) again. She had always been in my mind for *The World Unseen*. I did look at other actresses for Amina only because I didn't want to go back to what was comfortable for the wrong reasons. In the end, I thought Sheetal Sheth had the combination of vulnerability and strength that I wanted for the role.

W&H: *I Can't Think Straight* **is chock full of stereotypes and you really open up the conversation about culture and respect while challenging the stereotypes. Was that your intention?**

SS: Definitely. I wanted to set it within an Arab family. First of all, I don't think we get many depictions of upper class, well-educated Arabs, and having been a part of that world for a while through my partner, I was frankly horrified at what was said behind closed doors. I wasn't hearing that anywhere so I wanted to explore it a little bit. It's an issue for me that Palestine is not free and that they can't come to some kind of resolution on the situation. Both sides need to come to the table.

W&H: **You worked with many women on your film, which is quite unique.**

SS: There was a big difference between *The World Unseen* and *I Can't Think Straight*, which had a very male-centric team around that first investor.

W&H: **Was there a different experience on the sets?**

SS: *I Can't Think Straight* was not a good experience. Not because there were mostly men, but because they were just very chauvinistic. They were not remotely supportive of the vision. They seemed more interested in setting up their own projects instead of setting up the camera. It was a mess except for the director of photography. Working on *The World Unseen* was a dream by comparison. The majority of crew and cast attached themselves because they were passionate about the project and in a way, having everyone pull together on a thirty-day shoot gave all the crew a sense of responsibility and they rose to that beautifully. It was a pleasure.

W&H: **Do you think they didn't respect you because you were a woman or a new director or both?**

SS: I think so because they were "those kind of guys." There were a few exceptions, but they were mostly not supportive and I think it was partly being a new director, but mostly being a woman. None of them was experienced in film either. I felt it was just a strongly macho culture. It was very different on the second film where everybody was pulling together.

W&H: **I read that *The World Unseen* is partially based on your grandmother?**

SS: It's not actually my grandmother. The Miriam character is closer to my grandmother in terms of the isolated life but she never had the "opening up" experience, certainly not sexually. Amina was based on a real character at that time. All I kept hearing about is that she wore trousers, never got married, and drove taxis for a living. I thought how does someone like this exist at that time? That was how I came up with the back-story of her grandmother who was raped on her way from South Africa to India and raised Amina to be self-sufficient so she wouldn't go through the same thing. Also, Amina's father doesn't care what people say and I think this combination, together with her natural character, gave her the strength to live her own life.

I didn't want to make it a big issue that she is gay and in fact that's what tips her relationship with Miriam into romance. It's not about Amina's sexuality; it's about Miriam's journey to independence. I thought it would be nice to have a movie where a character is gay and it not the be-all and end-all.

W&H: **You have a production company with your partner. What do you have in development?**

SS: We have several projects at different stages—all with strong female characters. The next film is based on my second book, *Despite the Falling Snow,* and is set in Cold War Russia. It's a story of love and betrayal. An enigmatic young Russian woman takes an assignment spying on an idealistic politician and falls in love with him. Whether you can avoid betraying someone you love or your own beliefs is a major theme.

W&H: **Why do you think that we have such a hard time with films that star female protagonists?**

SS: In Europe, especially in France, they have strong women. I don't know, because it's unfathomable to me. I love women; I love female characters. I like good male characters, too, but women hold a special place for me—I find them endlessly fascinating. I don't have an answer for that because I can't relate. My dream is for this to be a complete nonissue in the near future!

Lone Scherfig

Date of Release (or festival premiere): 2009 Sundance Film Festival

Link to IMDb page: www.imdb.com/title/tt1174732

Link to Site: www.sonyclassics.com/aneducation

Link to Trailer: www.youtube.com/watch?v=qn9IMe5jmf0

BIO: Lone Scherfig was born in Copenhagen and studied film at the University of Copenhagen and the National Film School of Denmark. She has written and directed short films, radio dramas, and television series. *Italian for Beginners* (the fifth Danish Dogma film) received a FIPRESCI award and a Silver Bear Jury Prize at the Berlin International Film Festival, and the Robert Award for Best Original Screenplay from the Danish Film Academy. Other features include *The Birthday Trip* and *On Our Own*.

Her first English language film, *Wilbur Wants to Kill Himself*, received the FIPRESCI prize and a host of international film awards. Lone conceived the characters that formed the basis for Andrea Arnold's Cannes Jury Prize winning film *Red Road*.

Her latest film is *One Day*, adapted from the novel by David Nicholls. (Credit: *An Education* Official Website)

DESCRIPTION: *An Education* is a feminist coming-of-age story of Jenny (Carey Mulligan)—a too-smart, too-worldy-for-her-own-good young woman in 1961 in London when young women had few choices. The country is still living in a post-war mentality. The "Swinging '60s" haven't begun yet. What Jenny has going for her is that her father (Alfred Molina) has drilled it into her head that she must get a proper education in order to be successful. Jenny believes it and works hard for it.

Then she meets David (Peter Sarsgaard), an older con man who opens her world and offers her a different type of education. He takes her to concerts, makes up stories about people he knows, and not only enchants Jenny, but also her parents so much so that plan A for Jenny's education—university—is thrown out the window in favor of plan B—marriage. These plans of romance and enchantment continue until Jenny makes a devastating discovery.

An Education is about choices and how each choice has consequences. But it is also about how those choices teach us—give us an education, if you will—so that as we grow up maybe, just maybe, we will make different ones next time.

Interview Date: October 20, 2009

WOMEN AND HOLLYWOOD: **So here we are in 2009 and the issue of women directors is still a big issue. Do you believe that work-family balance is as big an issue for male directors as it is for female directors?**

LONE SCHERFIG: As a director you need to have such a strange combination of skills, and no one can have all of them. One is an ability to be able to leave home for a while, stay up very late, or do things that would harm your family life no matter what sex you are. And maybe it's easier for men to compromise more but it must be a big loss to them, as well. But the thing for me is that I started out very young and had my daughter quite late, so it meant I had a career that was strong enough. One regret is that I didn't have my child earlier and had more children. I'd encourage everyone to do that but you obviously have to pay a price for it.

W&H: **Another thing I read is that you said you make films to maintain the language, please explain.**

LS: In Denmark, we have a state supported system in order to maintain our language—that's how those films are financed. It's a privilege for a director because you are expected to do something that's not primarily commercial—quality is the first priority—and that has been really lovely for me because it has meant that I had chances I would not have been able to get in a different system. It's a handicap that those films cannot be seen by very many people; they would have to be subtitled like *Italian for Beginners.*

W&H: **Some of the strongest female voices in directing have come from places where there is state-sponsorship for films. Here in the United States, we don't have that system. Do you believe that the state-sponsored system has enabled you to have the type of career you have now?**

LS: Yes, I do. I think it's not just for women; it goes for anyone who is a minority when it comes to media access. If you want films—and media in general—that reflect the real world, you have to stay open for someone coming in the door to apply for that job, someone who is not an obvious candidate.

W&H: **Do you think it made a difference that there were two female producers on your film?**

LS: No. I know that they had thought that since the writer is a man that it might make sense to have a female director. But in general, it doesn't attract me to a job at all when someone says that. I am interested in projects where they want a good director rather than necessarily a female director. I'm sure all women say that. My films are not necessarily about my gender. The reason why I am privileged enough to say that is, thank God, there is a slightly older generation [of women] who have prepared that possibility for me. I am very thankful to the women who are ten to fifteen years older than I, who stood up for someone like me to get those possibilities.

W&H: **Which women directors do you mean?**

LS: Very often they are women academics, female politicians, film writers. It's not the directors. The directors I relate to the most are male. My mom would teach me to mend my dress and to cook like a proper mother and shared her love for the arts and films and literature; but it's women who are slightly younger (than her) who fought the battle for women. That combination is what I am really thankful for and that enriches my life immensely.

W&H: **There were so many different "educations" in the film. And so I wanted to ask you, which education do you feel impacted you the most?**

LS: I'm a bit like Jenny. I totally share the appetite that she had for learning that might not be in the syllabus. Once she knows and can define what she loves, the education seems to be something that's driven by appetite rather than duty or ambition. The things you read and the things you see because you love them are the easiest and the best education to get.

        The same thing happened to me when I was young. I found out that film was something I could make a career in and when I got to university, and later film school, and found myself surrounded by people who loved what I loved, that's when I really got an education and finally did all my homework because I loved it. That is a privilege. Loving things does not necessarily mean you have a talent for it. But I am trying to tell my own daughter that if she finds something that she loves to do that the money will come. That may be a false promise, because not everyone has that privileged choice.

W&H: **You talk a lot about your love for the character of David, played by Peter Sarsgaard. I found him to be a transitional figure because he opens doors to the coming revolution in terms of race and class and religion, and he provides all the educations and never gets schooled in anything. Why are you so fond of David?**

LS: That's a brilliant and interesting way you are putting it. I didn't think of that. I think, for me, the key to all the characters has been their relation to an education. That's how I started the conversations with all the actors. In David's case, he is someone who wants the life he could have had, if he had the education, which he did not have access to. He doesn't feel he is lying; he's just saying what he wants to say and what he believes is right at the moment. I know that's how Peter saw him, as well. Neither Peter nor I had any problems in liking him and I always feel that I want to defend David. You get seduced, the way Jenny and her parents are. Peter says that, when David is with Jenny, he can get the childhood he never had. That being said, Peter is so experienced for his age and the way he plays his cards. We shot the film out of sequence—of course—but the way more and more of David's flaws are revealed is really elegant. Peter is technically and structurally such a skilled actor but his acting is completely emotional and spontaneous and of the moment. He was on board the film before I was. It came as such a fringe benefit that I was able to work with the best actor.

W&H: **What is it like for women directors in Denmark?**

LS: Probably much better than anywhere else. I have directed the most commercial Scandinavian film—except, maybe, now *The Girl With the Dragon Tattoo*, which has done better. Susanne Bier, my friend and colleague, has directed the most commercial Danish film. She and I are much respected and we get many opportunities. They've let me experiment—sometimes to a degree of irresponsibility. It's our films that get into Sundance. We get huge support compared to other countries, but the money still ends up in the pockets of men.

W&H: **What do you mean?**

LS: It is still men who own all the equipment and the men who make the money, but there are a lot of female producers and production designers and directors in Denmark. In Sweden, there is a system where the state would add something like $200,000 to the budget if the director is a woman and we really disapprove of that. We think it is humiliating. Sweden is much more feminist and more political and less pragmatic and in Sweden you get a completely different kind of respect. But we just don't want that. When I read interviews with some of the other women directors coming out of Denmark, I see they react the same way. We want to work because we know how to do the work.

W&H: **Why do you think the film has touched such a nerve with people?**

LS: I'm hoping it's the integrity. That it's a film that is accessible and does invite you into a world where you haven't been and makes you think thoughts you haven't thought about. I am so happy that there is a space for this film. I have to thank the press since we really need your help in explaining what the film is about because it's not that easy to explain.

W&H: **Now that you are getting such great notices for your work, have you gotten a lot of offers for your next projects?**

LS: My only hope is that—since it looks like this film is going to land on both legs—this means I will get better scripts. My fuss is not where the script comes from or who produces it, but the content and the characters.

W&H: **Did you have to fight to get this script?**

LS: Yes. I had to fight pretty hard but it may be because I am Danish and not English. I didn't know the rules of the game. I don't sell myself very hard. I think that Nick Hornby (the film's writer) and I have something in common and that his novels and my films are related. The good thing about being foreign is that when people hire you as a foreigner, they expect that you will influence the film with something that comes from a different culture and that gives you more artistic freedom.

W&H: **Lastly, the obligatory Carey Mulligan question. Why has this young woman just taken off? Is it that she just seems such a natural?**

LS: She is a natural and the one main reason for casting her is that there is no phoniness about her. She's reached a point now where you can't say she doesn't have an acting education anymore—she's worked so hard. At that time (before we made the film), she had done very little. She makes good choices and is super disciplined when it comes to preparing. She's strong and has the talent to be able to carry a film, not just play a part. I don't think people will be disappointed when they see the film. It's tricky when there is such buzz around someone whose work you have not even seen yet. But I am so happy because the film gets so much more attention.

Céline Sciamma

FILM TITLE: *Water Lilies*

Date of Release (or festival premiere): 2007 Cannes Film Festival

Link to IMDb page: www.imdb.com/title/tt0869977

Link to Site: www.waterliliesmovie.co.uk

Link to Trailer: www.waterliliesmovie.co.uk/trailer

BIO: Céline Sciamma was born in 1978 and grew up in the Paris suburbs. After obtaining a master's degree in French literature, she took screenwriting courses at the French film school La Femis. Céline's first feature film, *Water Lilies*, was selected for the Cannes/Un Certain Regard (2007) and has screened at more than thirty festivals worldwide including Toronto, London, New York, Tokyo, and Rotterdam. Acclaimed by the film critics, the film won the prestigious French Louis-Delluc award. *Tomboy* is her second feature film. (Credit: *Tomboy* Official Website)

DESCRIPTION: Set in the competitive world of synchronized swimming, *Water Lillies* is a brilliantly observed portrait of female adolescence. The film centers around three fifteen-year-old girls who experience first love in very different ways. *Water Lillies* is the directorial debut of twenty-seven-year-old Céline Sciamma and stars newcomers Pauline Acquart, Louise Blachère, Adèle Haenel, and Warren Jacquin. Premiering at the 2007 Cannes Film Festival Un Certain Regard, Sciamma and her young cast were widely hailed as among the most talented newcomers to emerge from the festival. (Credit: *Water Lillies* Official Website)

Interview Date: May 16, 2008

WOMEN AND HOLLYWOOD: There are so few films that realistically deal with girls coming of age that your film is like a breath of fresh air. Why do you think this is a topic that is not explored more when boys' coming-of-age films are so common?

CÉLINE SCIAMMA: Cinema has been celebrating women for a century now but men have mostly done the talking. I think you have to be a woman to be truly genuine and committed to the subject and to tell that particular story, especially when it comes to coming-of-age stories. Hopefully, the rise of a generation of women filmmakers means that the topic will be explored.

W&H: You said that it's a tough job to be a girl. What do you mean by that?

CS: It's a tough job because of the many things that are expected of girls that are often contradictory. Being strong but hiding your strength, being in charge but not being officially the boss. It's a tough job because girls live in a man's world.

W&H: Synchronized swimming is such a bizarre feminine activity. It's hard and athletic so you need to train but it's also about beauty and smiling and looking pretty. Why did you choose to use synchronized swimming as the focal point of so many of the film's activities?

CS: The thing that interested me mostly about synchronized swimming is the way it tells a lot about the girls' condition. Synchronized swimmers are soldiers who look like dolls. On the surface they have to pretend that they don't suffer, with all the makeup and the fake smiles, whereas underwater/underneath they painfully struggle with the element. Synchronized swimming is about pretending; it's about hiding the pain and the sacrifice you go through to be officially gracious. Those two levels you can find in ordinary teenagehood.

W&H: You said that Floriane's character gave you the opportunity to explore the tragedy of being a pretty girl. What do you mean by that?

CS: Films usually celebrate the beauty of girls like it's an achievement. But being beautiful is an issue just as being unattractive is. It's something you have to deal with, something you have to face. The lust it generates. It's one of the problems of femininity.

W&H: There seems to be a disconnect (especially here in the United States) between the taboo of discussing the reality of girls' sexuality and the constant push towards sexualizing girls through clothing, ads, and images in the media. Do you have any thoughts on that?

CS: That's an illustration of the tough job of being a girl! That's the kind of contradiction girls have to deal with everyday. They have to live up to the fantasy and in the meantime be discreet about their feelings and their urges. They must trigger desire but they don't have the right to express theirs.

W&H: **Why did you pick the title *Water Lilies*?**

CS: I didn't pick it myself actually. It's the international title. The original French title is *Naissance des Pieuvres*, which means "Birth of the Octopuses." Rather different as you can see! But I really like the title *Water Lilies*; it's smoother than the French title and it has that poetic feeling. One can say that the three characters are like water lilies, beautiful flowers on the surface but hiding deep roots . . .

W&H: **Do you think it's easier for women directors in Europe, and if yes, why?**

CS: I don't know if it's easier, but this year—and I hope it's not a coincidence—a lot of the first-time French directors were women. France has a tradition of women filmmakers that really began in the '90s and keeps blooming. But one cannot talk about Europe. I don't know any women directors in Italy, nor Spain . . . When I came to New York for the release, film teachers at New York University were telling me that their most promising students were women. Something might be happening here . . .

W&H: **Do you think your film is a feminist film?**

CS: When a public woman is asked if she is a feminist, she tends to answer "no," as if it was some kind of an insult. I think the film is feminist. That doesn't mean that the film is made for a female audience, that doesn't mean that it's an exposé. It's a story that I wanted to be generous, catchy, and touching. It's feminist because it goes beyond the fantasy, because it goes against the folklore of teenage girls in cotton underwear. Water Lilies goes in the locker rooms of girls not to eye-drop, but to see the crude reality. It allows everyone in the audience to experience what it's like to be a girl.

Photo Credit: Eliza Truitt

Lynn Shelton

FILM TITLE: *Humpday*

Date of Release (or festival premiere): 2009 Sundance Film Festival

Link to IMDb page: www.imdb.com/title/tt1334537

Link to Site: www.humpdayfilm.com

Link to Trailer: www.humpdayfilm.com

BIO: Lynn Shelton grew up in Seattle, studying acting, painting, poetry, and photography. After a decade spent acting for the stage, she attended the MFA program in photography at the School of Visual Arts in New York City. She then spent a decade learning the ins and outs of cinema as an experimental and documentary filmmaker and as an editor, before writing and directing her first feature-length film upon invitation from The Film Company, a nonprofit film studio. The result, *We Go Way Back*, premiered at SLAMDANCE 2006, where it picked up the Grand Jury Award for Best Narrative Feature and the Award for Best Cinematography.

Her second feature film, *My Effortless Brilliance*, premiered at SXSW 2008 and screened at a bevy of festivals across the country. The film was awarded the Special Jury Prize for Excellence in Direction at the Atlanta Film Festival and was picked up for distribution by IFC Films. *Humpday*, Shelton's third feature starring Mark Duplass and Joshua Leonard, premiered at Sundance in 2009. She has also directed an episode of *Mad Men* and *Your Sister's Sister*, starring Emily Blunt, Rosemarie DeWitt, and Mark Duplass that was released in 2012. Her latest film *Touchy Feely* premiered at the 2013 Sundance Film Festival. (Credit: Lynn Shelton website)

DESCRIPTION: *Humpday* written and directed by Lynn Shelton was one of those movies that came out of Sundance this year with a lot of buzz. The premise sounded funny but stupid: two old college friends, Ben and Andrew, played by Mark Duplass and Joshua Leonard— straight guys—decide to make a porn flick together. My first thought was another stupid bromance.

This movie is anything but stupid. Shelton takes on some of the biggest taboo issues in a way that really makes you think. She takes on sexuality—male sexuality—and while the idea of making the film might have started as a joke in a drunken haze, it takes on a lot of loaded issues which I found brilliant. These guys ask themselves if they could really have sex with each other and if they are even think- ing about it, does that mean they could be gay? The film layers on other life issues like am I on the right path? Did I just settle? And the ultimate question, do I know who I am? The third player in the film is Ben's wife, Anna (Alycia Delmore), a woman who thought she knew her husband but when she finds out about the film, is forced to look at her husband and herself differently.

This is a really good movie. I love that here is a woman exploring issues about guys in such a funny, smart, and respectful way that it will hopefully continue to dispel the fallacy that women can only direct films about women.

Interview Date: July 8, 2009

WOMEN AND HOLLYWOOD: Why did you want to tell this story?

LYNN SHELTON: Good drama (and comedy) often comes from the simple act of placing characters in a situation that is neither usual nor comfortable for them. That's what *Humpday* does, at its most basic level. And I knew that placing these particular characters into this particular uncomfortable situation was going to allow for an exploration of all kinds of things that interest me: the limitations of friendship (specifically male friendship), the nuances of marital relationships, the various guises we don depending on the context (at home with our mates vs. flying solo at a wild swinging party, for example), coming to grips with the fact that the image we have of ourselves doesn't necessarily jibe with who we are in actuality . . . Not to mention issues of sexual politics: the low grade homophobia of the average, well-meaning straight guy, the rigidity/fluidity of the boundaries of our sexual identity.

W&H: **Your film is so funny yet really touches on some important cultural issues like masculinity and sexuality. How important was keeping it funny and light?**

LS: Although humor is present in every one of my films, it has always been used as a way to make the darker, heavier stuff in my stories more palatable. I never set out to make *Humpday* a comedy. We played every scene straight. I mean, we were not unaware of the potential for laughter, but we really didn't think about it on set. The scene in which Ben's wife, Anna, finds out the true nature of the "art project" gets a huge amount of laughter in the theater (albeit awkward, anxiety-ridden laughter), but shooting that scene was incredibly intense; it was by far the hardest, most serious day on set.

W&H: **This summer both you and Kathryn Bigelow are directing films that we don't see women direct very often. Stories about guys. Why do you think that is such an issue when it is never an issue when men direct stories about women?**

LS: Hmm, can I be obvious and say there is probably a double standard for male and female directors? Sadly, I think that's actually the case. And it probably stems from the fact that there are proportionately fewer women directors that each project is perhaps more closely scrutinized for its content. But maybe it's more equal than we realize . . . I've read that Mike Leigh gets asked all the time about why he makes movies about women (and very good ones at that) and his very apt answer is that he doesn't make movies about women or about men . . . he makes movies about people.

W&H: **I have described your film as a bromance without the typical misogyny since there is no overt hatred toward women in the film. How important was it to you that Anna be an important piece of the story?**

LS: It was vitally, VITALLY important to me. It was also vitally important to me for this film not be a homophobic one, by the way. But yes, back to Anna: I am as proud of her character and her role in the film as I am of any other element in it. She so easily could have been a cipher, or a character only there to serve Ben's character. I didn't want her to be that, and I didn't want her to be a harpy or a doormat either. I wanted her to be smart and sympathetic and as fully fleshed out and complicated as the two guys in the film, even though she doesn't get the same amount of screen time. It was important to me as a matter of principle (how sick am I of the cardboard cut-out ancillary "girlfriend" or "wife" character in male-driven movies?) but also because if you don't care about Anna and the relationship between her and Ben, the movie simply wouldn't work. There would be no stakes, no tension, no emotional investment as to whether or not the boys do it and how the whole story unfolds.

W&H: **Explain to people what the "upside-down" model of filmmaking is and why it works so well for you.**

LS: After experiencing the traditional model of filmmaking with my first feature, I wanted to create a totally actor-centered atmosphere on set with my second feature film. It was really an experiment to see if I could capture a level of naturalism that would be so high, it would almost feel like a documentary. So instead of writing predetermined dialogue for characters that I thought up in my head, I decided to start with the people I wanted to work with and then handcraft characters designed just for them. I invite the actors in very early on in the process, when the film is still a loose story, because they will be heavily involved in the development of their own characters and I need to know who those characters are before I can cement how they will behave in each scene. The film evolves organically from that point on. By the time we get to the set, everyone has a detailed back-story and they are all intimately acquainted with their own characters. Instead of a proper script, we have a detailed outline of all the scenes. We know the point of every scene, and the emotional map of every scene, but the actors come up with the actual words on their own. With the right casting (as well as a very high level of skill in the editing room), I have found that this kind of highly structured, highly directed improvisation can give me both the naturalism that I crave and the structure that I love.

W&H: **What are you working on next?**

LS: I'm shooting "$5 Cover Seattle," a music-based web series being produced by MTV. It was the brainchild of another independent filmmaker, Craig Brewer, whose original version, "$5 Cover Memphis," can be seen on MTV.com right now. I'm very excited about the project because it's a great fit for my creative style, plus I get to work intimately with a bunch of sexy rock stars, pretty much a dream come true.

Photo Credit: Bart Babinski

Agnieszka Wojtowicz-Vosloo

FILM TITLE: *After.Life*

Date of Release (or festival premiere): 2009 AFI Film Festival

Link to IMDb Page: www.imdb.com/title/tt0838247

Link to Site: www.afterlifethefilm.com

Link to Trailer: www.afterlifethefilm.com/site.html#/video

BIO: Polish-American filmmaker, Agnieszka Wojtowicz-Vosloo, studied film at Tisch School of the Arts at New York University. Her debut short film, *Pâté*, premiered at the 2001 Sundance Film Festival and won several prestigious awards. In 2008, *Filmmaker Magazine* named Wojtowicz-Vosloo as one of the twenty-five New Faces of Independent Film. In 2004, she collaborated with Laurie Anderson on the acclaimed *O Zlozony/O Composite*, a multi-media project for the Paris Opera Ballet with choreography by Trisha Brown, based on Czeslaw Milosz's poem "O Zlozony." The piece premiered at the Opera Garnier in Paris in December 2004.

Her debut feature, *After.Life*, a psychological horror thriller starring Liam Neeson, Christina Ricci, and Justin Long, premiered at the AFI Film Festival in Los Angeles in 2009. Agnieszka is currently in pre-production for her next feature to be shot in Japan in 2013.

DESCRIPTION: *After.Life* asks the question: What is death? For those interested in horror/supernatural flicks, this might be one for you. The film stars Christina Ricci as a young woman who doesn't believe she is dead after a violent car crash. The undertaker (Liam Neeson) communes with the dead, preparing them for the afterlife. But the question the film attempts to answer is, "Is she really dead?"

Interview Date: April 9, 2010

WOMEN AND HOLLYWOOD: This is your first film and you have an A-list cast. How did that happen?

AGNIESZKA WOJTOWICZ-VOSLOO: They responded to the material. It's really as simple as that. If you create strong characters then actors will always respond. They like original characters that are a bit different, a bit edgier. Liam Neeson was my dream for the part of Eliot, a mysterious funeral director, who seems to possess the ability to transition the dead but who might actually have much darker motives. Liam responded to the script and to what I was trying to say with the story. He liked the idea of posing questions about life and death. We met. We had a creative connection. He wanted to hear my vision for the film and had lots of questions and ideas. We spoke about everything from his character to the colors and textures I wanted to use to evoke the mood and the atmosphere of unease and eeriness.

It was the same with Christina Ricci. A number of actresses were interested in the role because frankly there's still such a lack of interesting roles for women. Christina was intrigued by the character. She was fascinated by the idea that maybe our consciousness remains with us after we die and you're able to reflect on your life, which in Anna's case wasn't fully lived, to say the least. Even though *After.Life* is a psychological thriller, for Christina, it was a character piece of sorts. Again, it was all about the material, a challenging and unusual role and a shared vision for the film.

W&H: **I noticed that there are several people credited as writers of the film. What was your process of writing?**

AWV: I wrote *After.Life* with my partner, Paul Vosloo, and a good friend in Warsaw, Jakub Korolczuk. The process was interesting and very rewarding, working with partners forces you to push yourself. You can't get away with lazy writing. They pounce on you straight away. We'd all write scenes then compare notes and agree on the best version. It was truly collaborative. The reason I became a filmmaker is because I love collaboration. The process was very gratifying.

W&H: **After your short film *Pâté* played at Sundance, you said you received several potential scripts to direct but you didn't take any of them and realized you had to create your own material. What types of scripts were you offered, and do you think that it's more common for women to go the writer/director route?**

AWV: There were scripts like *Dirty Dancing 2* as well as the usual rom-coms and coming-of-age stories, which is not really me. Then there were the ODAs (Open Director Assignments), which were mostly average—and when a good script came along, it was quickly snapped up by A-List directors. That's when I realized I had to write my own material. By turning down the offers, I definitely took a longer and more difficult road but at the same time it was so much more satisfying. Looking back, it was the best decision I made.

Is it more common for women to go the writer/director route? I don't know. There's definitely a shortage of good material out there and the established directors who get the best material tend to be male.

W&H: **What inspired you to create this story?**

AWV: I always had this image in my head of a woman on a slab and a mortician standing over her. The woman who should be dead speaks, and the mortician calmly responds to her. It was a powerful idea to me. I've always been terrified, but also morbidly curious about death. My father died when I was ten years old, and it had a huge impact on my life and made me wonder what really happens to us after we die.

I wanted to explore those themes in the film. What happens to your body after you die? What happens to your soul? Or even what stages your consciousness goes through? I wanted to go beyond this idea of death and look at the human experience as a whole. If someone is physically alive but moves along like an empty vessel, is that person truly alive? Ultimately, *After.Life* is not just about death but also about life.

W&H: **What was the most challenging thing about the directing process and what was the most rewarding thing?**

AWV: The most challenging thing? Always wishing you had more
        time. On *After.Life* we all knew going in that this was a very
        ambitious project to be shot in such a short time (twenty-five
        days). Way too ambitious. We knew we'd have to work very fast
        with limited takes and coverage. Everyone worked extremely
        hard to realize my vision, but ultimately we had to find creative
        ways to scale down certain things. I storyboarded every shot
        and had a very specific vision for each scene, so it was frustrat-
        ing to have to compromise. But then the one thing I learned is
        that filmmaking is all about compromise. And I mean it in a
        good sense of the word.

        There were so many rewarding things about making *After.*
        Life. First, the entire journey from writing the first scene of the
        script to actually having your first feature released in cinemas.
        I've learned so much every step of the way. Also having the
        opportunity to tell a story I was so passionate about with three
        extraordinary actors was extremely rewarding. They were so
        passionate and committed to the project, and we had the best
        working relationship a director can dream of.

W&H: **What's next for you?**

AWV: A vacation. There are a number of projects I'm looking at plus
        I've almost completed another script. After we debuted *After.*
        Life at AFI last November, I received a couple of directing offers
        that I must say are a lot better quality than what I was offered
        after my short premiered at Sundance. Right now my main
        focus is seeing *After.Life* through until it gets into theaters this
        week and then I can focus on my next project. But I definitely
        want to get back on set soon so it looks like my next project is
        going to be someone else's material.

W&H: **What advice do you have for female directors?**

AWV: It's tough out there. Period. There is a lot of competition and it's not enough to just be talented. You've got to work extremely hard, sacrifice many things, and go through a lot of rejections. It's all part of the process. And unfortunately it's a lot tougher for women. My advice is don't let yourself be pigeonholed into being a "female" director. You have to be as aggressive and as assertive as men. Ironically, our natural tendency to be collaborative and sharing makes us ideal filmmakers—but terrible at playing the Hollywood power game.

Photo Credit: Sven Arnstein

Susanna White

FILM TITLE: *Nanny McPhee Returns*

Date of Release (or festival premiere): August 20, 2010

Link to IMDb Page: www.imdb.com/title/tt1415283

Link to Site: www.universalstudiosentertainment.com/nanny-mcphee-returns

Link to Trailer: www.youtube.com/watch?v=54xMw6eouOM

BIO: BAFTA Award-winning director Susanna White began her filmmaking career making documentaries for the BBC, such as *The Gypsies Are Coming*. She attended Oxford University on scholarship and then studied film and television production at the University of California, Los Angeles, on a Fulbright.

White won widespread praise in 2005 for her direction of the BBC's acclaimed drama series *Bleak House* based on Charles Dickens' novel. She directed another drama series for the BBC the following season—*Jane Eyre*, which earned several awards nominations, including an Emmy nomination for Best Director Miniseries. White directed the first three and final episode of HBO's *Generation Kill*. She has also directed the television series *Parade's End* and HBO's *Boardwalk Empire*.

DESCRIPTION: When Nanny McPhee (Emma Thompson) appears at the farmhouse door of busy young mother Isabel Green (Maggie Gyllenhaal), she discovers that Mrs. Green's children are in an all-out household war with their two spoiled city cousins. Relying on everything from a flying motorcycle and a statue that comes to life, to a tree-climbing piglet and an elephant that turns up in the oddest places, Nanny McPhee uses her magic to teach the children five valuable lessons, the most important of which is learning how to get along. (Credit: *Nanny McPhee Returns* Official Website)

Interview Date: August 20, 2010

WOMEN AND HOLLYWOOD: How did you get the script for the film?

SUSANNA WHITE: I was sent it. I can remember the day very clearly. I was out in Africa. I was researching the moment when the American Marines crossed the border from Kuwait into Iraq (for *Generation Kill*). And I came in, washed the sand off me, and was completely transported. I fell in love with the writing. It's such a departure from what I've done before. I really engaged with the material, mainly with the character of Mrs. Green, a mom who is desperately trying to hold it all together—do a job, run the house, look after her kids, and care for the old people in the village—and not really coping and in desperate need of a nanny. I thought, although loosely set in World War II, it felt like a contemporary story I wanted to tell.

W&H: **Why was it so attractive to you since this was such a big departure from what you are known for?**

SW: I had been trying forever to break into features for as long as I can remember. I started making films when I was eight years old and it was a long journey. And here was an opportunity to make a big studio film with a really good script. And I knew we could attract a level of cast that was going to be fantastic. The other big thing for me was that it involved a lot of CGI (Computer-Generated Imagery), which is an area that I really love working in. So this checked many of the boxes for me in terms of what I wanted to do and it felt like an exciting opportunity.

W&H: **You've done documentaries. You've worked in television. Why did it take so long to break into directing features?**

SW: I guess for a long time I thought it was my problem. That maybe there was some quality in me that was holding me back. And it was really making *Generation Kill*, because to me, whether I'm creating World War II London or the world of the Marines in Iraq, it's about creating a world. And then it's different in some sense. But clearly, other people saw it as incredibly significant that I directed a TV series about an all-male world. And it made me realize that there actually was a whole level of sexism going on. People in general didn't think anything about a man directing something on what might be a female subject. But people saw it as very significant that here was a woman doing a piece of work about an all-male world. And that's when I really woke up and thought people really do see me, not just as a director, but as a woman who is directing. I think it was very significant that Kathryn Bigelow won the Oscar for directing *The Hurt Locker*. But people saw that as some kind of major achievement. Whereas, to me, *The Piano* (directed by Jane Campion) is just as much of an achievement.

W&H: **Can you talk about how you got the gig on *Generation Kill*?**

SW: It had been submitted to Kevin McDonald who is represented by the same agent as me in London. Kevin wasn't available to do it and my agent called me and said that these great David Simon scripts were coming and that I should take a look at it. I am a big David Simon fan. I read it and met with him and we really connected. This was a movie about exploring characters under pressure. And I really enjoyed doing the action but that wasn't the main thing that made me want to tell the story. We also connected in that we both were really interested in using a combination of actors and non-actors. With my documentary background and David's background—coming out of *The Corner* and *The Wire*—we had a very similar philosophy about not wanting to see *any* acting, for it to feel *very* real. And finally, he was a big *Bleak House* fan. He has been compared to Dickens before and I think he really liked this idea of the woman who directed *Bleak House* to direct *Generation Kill*. I have to say, directing that series was one of the most positive experiences of my career.

W&H: **What was your biggest take-away from that?**

SW: I think to realize I could probably do anything. Not to be afraid anymore. I think it gave me a whole lot of confidence because I went into that never having done action, CGI, I had never done a scene with thirty-five characters in it! Doing all that, way in the middle of Africa, in really tough conditions in the desert—it made me think, "If I can do this, I can probably try my hand at anything."

W&H: **Now that you've done your first feature, have you lined up the
       second one?**

SW: I'm working on various things. I'm having a fantastic time at
       the moment working with Tom Stoppard on a series for HBO
       called *Parade's End*. It's basically one great big novel divided
       into various parts that tells the story of a marriage around the
       time of the First World War. It's a big saga. We are working on
       that together and that's about to cast at the moment. And then
       I'm also working on a thriller by John le Carré.

W&H: **So you weren't pigeonholed back in the girl world after Nanny
       McPhee?**

SW: That was important to me. It was interesting doing the junkets
       because a lot of people were saying it's great having a woman
       directing this movie and asking what it was like working with
       the children. And I absolutely loved doing *Nanny McPhee* on so
       many levels, partially because I really wanted to make a movie
       for my kids and my family. However, I was really conscious
       of not wanting to be pigeonholed in that way. It's been great
       because I've been sent all kinds of things, and it's very exciting.

W&H: **Is there a difference between directing features and television?**

SW: I think directing features is just better. During my whole career
       in television, I had been dreaming up ideas, and people would
       say that it's a great idea but too expensive. On this, Eric Fellner
       at Working Title was so encouraging to me. He said, "just
       look at every scene and think how to make the best possible
       version of that scene. Look at the ideas in that script and think
       how to make them the greatest cinema moment you can." For
       instance, Emma had written a scene where a pig dives into a
       pond and comes out the other side. And I was in my bath and
       thought, "What if I did a whole Busby Berkeley set piece here
       with synchronized swimming and pigs?" And I went back to

Emma and asked what she thought of the idea and Lindsay Doran, the producer, really liked it because she was an Esther Williams fan. I suddenly realized I found this thing where I expected everyone to say no but instead people were saying, "Wow, that's great! Can you think of more stuff?" And then I dreamt up a magical harvest, and other big set pieces.

Then there is the opportunity to get an A-list cast. That was very exciting to me. The casting director had asked who I wanted to play Lord Gray and I said Ralph Fiennes and she said, "Yeah, but who else." I said I want Ralph Fiennes because he's the right person for that role. And we offered it to him and we got him. And similarly, I thought who would be the ideal father to come over the hill and I thought Ewan McGregor. I know Ewan's agent quite well and we floated it past her and we got Ewan McGregor. It was thrilling. On the other hand, I think television is a very exciting place, and certainly, with HBO all the boundaries are shifting. With people like Kate Winslet doing work for HBO, that's one of the reasons I'm so excited about working on this Tom Stoppard project, because it's a really great long-form drama. So that's the right setting for that piece of work. I think we're at a very exciting time in terms of the whole CGI world, and the 3D world and all the technology really excite me.

W&H: **What advice do you have for someone who wants to break into directing?**

SW: It took me a really long time. The only thing that kept me going . . . I guess I just had it inside me very early on and knew that this was what I had to do. It was a long hard struggle for me, even though I was lucky, because I got the Fulbright scholarship to go to film school at UCLA. After finishing at UCLA, it was seven years before I got a break. But I didn't give up. I think my best advice to people who want to direct is not to give up. At the moment, you can make things very cheaply. So keep making things. That's the best way to learn. By watching a lot of stuff and having a go. You don't need to make things on a big budget. The best ideas are free. I think it's about having faith.

W&H: **What has Kathryn Bigelow's Oscar win meant to you?**

SW: I hope that it is going to make it easier for people coming up now. I feel very lucky. I had a long career in television and now I've made a big scale feature, but it wasn't straightforward for me to get there. And I hope that for the young women coming through now that it's going to be easier—it will be a more level playing field. It will be talent that comes through, regardless of whether you're male or female, and I really hope that this Oscar put some big cracks in the glass ceiling.

W&H: **Why has the film *The Piano* influenced you above all other movies?**

SW: I think there is a very female sensibility behind that film. It's a very delicate, balanced, nuanced, and emotional story. And I can remember very clearly being at that movie with the man who became my husband and he did not get it. And still to this day, he cannot get why I got so excited about it and why I remain so excited about it. It was a very female story, brilliantly told. And I think everything about that movie worked. It's incredibly visual. I can still remember the shots of the big dress under the water. And the performances are so strong. It's unbelievably sexy and the score is just divine. It works on every level. I guess there are many movies that have influenced me but that one showed me a different way of making films. It's like hearing music being played but it's not in the pitch your voice fits in with. And, suddenly, there was something in my register that resonated for me.

Photo Credit: Joan Carr-Wiggin

Joan Carr-Wiggin

FILM TITLE: *A Previous Engagement*

Date of Release (or festival premiere): May 9, 2008

Link to IMDb Page: www.imdb.com/title/tt0411234

Link to Site: www.apreviousengagement.com

Link to Trailer: www.apreviousengagement.com

BIO: Joan Carr-Wiggin entered the film industry following a career as an
economist. She first wrote and directed the micro-budget comedy-drama
Honeymoon, starring Thomas Cavanagh and Pascale Bussières. She then wrote
and directed *A Previous Engagement*, starring Juliet Stevenson, Tcheky Karyo,
and Daniel Stern. Her latest film, *If I Were You*, stars Academy Award winner
Marcia Gay Harden, Leonor Watling, and Aidan Quinn. *If I Were You* is
a play-within-a-film, in which Harden plays Lear.

DESCRIPTION: When Seattle librarian Julia Reynolds talks her
unadventurous husband into a family vacation on the beautiful
Mediterranean island of Malta she has a secret agenda: a date made
twenty-five years earlier with her first love. But when the sexy
Frenchman actually shows up, insisting she's his true love, she discovers
a side of her husband she never suspected. The flat-footed insurance
man sets out in search of his own Malta romance, and is soon dancing
the salsa with an ex-chorus girl. In a movie for anyone who has ever
wondered what might have been, Julia must choose between the
husband she never really knew and the man she's dreamt of for twenty-
five years. (Credit: *A Previous Engagement* Official Website)

Interview Date: May 9, 2008

WOMEN AND HOLLYWOOD: What made you decide to write this story?

JOAN CARR-WIGGIN: I really wanted to tell a story about an older
woman taking control of her life. Not in the "she realizes
taking care of her family is the most important thing when she
becomes terminally ill" way. I see so many fascinating, funny,
and complicated older women living great lives but I don't see
women like that in films.

W&H: Did you know that you would be directing it when you wrote it?

JCW: Yes. That influenced the script. I don't think I'd enjoy direct-ing something too depressing. I write a wide range of scripts, I even wrote a sci-fi one once, which was a lot of fun, and I've written some very dramatic pieces, but I'm only interested in directing comedy. Preston Sturges is my favorite director, and I agree with the theme of his wonderful movie, *Sullivan's Travels*. Watching comedy makes life a little easier for people.

W&H: Most women filmmakers struggle to get financing for their films, but you seem to have had an easier time with it. Why do you think that's the case and what secrets can you share with other women looking for financing?

JCW: It's really hard to finance any kind of character-based film in Hollywood, not just one about women. One of our biggest advantages is that my husband, David Gordian, who produced the film, raises our financing in Canada and Europe, which are much more welcoming of women directors and character-based films than the American system. And the less money you need, the more freedom you have as a filmmaker. We're only interested in doing smaller, character driven films that feature performances rather than stunts and explosions. We have no desire to make a number one film at the box office. We just try to make a movie we'll enjoy ourselves. But Hollywood always wants to maximize gross revenues, even if the budget and the advertising costs wipe out their profits. It's a "bigger is better" mentality, and we just don't share it at all.

W&H: The line that resonates the most in the film is: "If people really knew who their mothers really were, the world would end." Why do you think it resonates so much?

JCW: It's one of those things everyone knows is true but no one ever talks about. I think most of us, as we get older, start to glimpse

that our mothers were much more complicated than we realized and we often regret not getting to know the real woman
underneath.

W&H: **Why do you think it's so difficult to get films about women
over forty made?**

JCW: There's a tendency in Hollywood to see films that have a young
and male sensibility as universal, and to see films that have an
older and female sensibility as only appealing to a niche. But
I've discovered that *A Previous Engagement* strikes a chord
with a lot of men, as well as women. So their premise just isn't
accurate. Part of the problem is that even when Hollywood
does make a film about an older woman, it often ends up
presenting an absurd caricature instead of a real woman, so of
course the film fails. And then Hollywood uses its failure as
an excuse not to finance interesting and promising films about
older women. But I was an economist before I was a filmmaker,
so I know there are many economic models, which can allow
films to be made and distributed. I think smart filmmakers
should just turn their backs on Hollywood. It operates on a
business model which functions, fairly efficiently, for the delivery of simplistic movies for the lowest common denominator.
And sometimes I enjoy those movies myself. But usually I
don't, and I would never want to direct one.

W&H: **Why do you think that the climate is so hostile to women
directors?**

JCW: Sexism is the short answer, and that explains a great deal
of it. Women make up about 6 percent of film directors, so,
proportionally, there are actually more women law partners,
politicians, and even astronauts, than directors. The fact that
Hollywood lags so far behind other industries helps to explain
why they continue to make movies that don't show women

accurately. And they use absurd excuses to resist change, such as the myth that directing is a difficult job for mothers. Except for during the actual filming, which is a small part of the overall job, the hours are flexible and a lot of work can be done from home. And of course no one talks about directing being too demanding a job for fathers. But I'm optimistic that things will start to get better for women directors with the rise of digital cinema and the Internet, which are both breaking down the entire economic model of the Hollywood production and distribution system. The world is changing in wonderful, exciting ways, even if Hollywood isn't.

W&H: **What advice would you give to other women filmmakers?**

JCW: Watch great movies, and remember that once you get past the financing struggles, actors and crew people are really accepting of women directors. *A Previous Engagement* was an absolute joy to make. And be persistent.

Photo Credit: Johnnie Shand-Kydd

Sam Taylor-Wood

FILM TITLE: *Nowhere Boy*

Date of Release (or festival premiere): 2009 London Film Festival

Link to IMDb Page: www.imdb.com/title/tt1266029

Link to Trailer: www.youtube.com/watch?v=WzvS78qO0uI

BIO: Sam Taylor-Wood is a filmmaker, visual artist, and photographer. She began her career in fine art and then branched into multi-screen video in 1994 with her piece *Killing Time*, which depicted four people miming an opera score. She created a video portrait of soccer legend David Beckham—shot in a single take. Other pieces include *Prelude in Air*, *Breach (Girl and Ennuch)*, *Still Life*, and *The Last Century*.

Nowhere Boy is her first feature film, for which she was nominated for a BAFTA.

DESCRIPTION: *Nowhere Boy*, Sam Taylor-Wood's biopic of teenage John Lennon, displays how Lennon was shaped by the two women in his life. His mother, Julia (Anne-Marie Duff) is the woman who could not raise him but helped him develop his love for music, and Aunt Mimi (Kristin Scott Thomas) is the woman who took him in, made him feel safe, and raised him as her own.

Interview Date: October 7, 2010

WOMEN AND HOLLYWOOD: Congratulations on the film. My mother was a fanatic John Lennon fan. I think you're going to talk to a big generation of women who were so into these guys.

SAM TAYLOR-WOOD: I felt that when I was making it. One of the few times I saw my mother cry was when Lennon died, and the other time was when Elvis died.

W&H: Why did you believe you were the right director for this film?

STW: I don't know. I read a lot of material, and this was the first I read that really shook me and made me feel something. Also, it was a story about someone I thought I knew so well but realized I didn't know the story at all. I felt that in that sense it was worth telling. This story just shook me so hard—I remember

closing the last pages of the script and crying, and just thinking that I have to make this film.

W&H: **You were lucky to have a mentor in the late director Anthony
Minghella. What do you remember as the best piece of advice
he gave you that you always keep with you?**

STW: He sent me this message that just said, "You did great and now
don't rest on your laurels." In other words, get back out there
and do it again and do it better. And that's what I kept in my
head. And really, it was his confidence that kept me going. It
wasn't necessarily one piece of advice so much as his telling me
that I can do this—that it is absolutely within you, and just go
ahead, just do it.

W&H: **Mimi and Julia were so important to John. Talk a little about
the importance of these women and the performances you
were able to get from these extraordinary actresses.**

STW: I felt they played an extraordinary part in Lennon's life, as
a mother would. And I felt that the two of them somehow
influenced him in different ways. I think Aunt Mimi was very
cultured, and she encouraged him to read authors like Oscar
Wilde and to look at art, paintings, and taught him about Van
Gogh. On the other hand, Julia was much more musically
based and she taught him how to play the banjo and taught
him about rock n' roll. So you have these two powerful influ-
ences that created the Lennon that we knew.

W&H: **I got a sense that Julia was mentally ill. It is never acknowledged in the film or even in the notes of the film, but she was
clearly a manic-depressive.**

STW: It was difficult. We're dealing with a very sensitive issue. There
are surviving family members. It's an issue that was never
diagnosed, so we can't assume too much. At the same time,

we go along with character traits we were told about. We have to look at it in the sense that here was a woman who had lost her son. She then had a daughter, and that daughter was taken away, as well. This might explain some of the mannerisms. And maybe, without making assumptions, and without knowing any diagnosis, some post-natal depression would be a possibility, or a depression of sorts—that any woman would have had under those circumstances. It was a difficult thing to try and convey this without making too many assumptions. In those days, something like a postpartum depression wouldn't have been recognized.

W&H: **What was it like, directing a film about such a force of nature and such a beloved individual? There are not many people who are as iconic as John Lennon.**

STW: It was difficult only at one stage. At first, I just went at it and thought I've got to look at this as a coming-of-age story, of a boy turning into a man with a love triangle and the struggle within that. There are enough elements there that can lead me away from the icon and keep me on a different path. However, as you're going down the path there are little reminders about *who* the story is about. And then, one great big reminder at the end. I think it was important for me to just keep focused in that way, so I didn't get too overwhelmed. When I went up to Liverpool for location hunting, that's when it really became clear to me that I was dealing with someone pretty spectacular and that I couldn't mess it up because there are too many people who love and adore him. I had to make sure I keep the full spectrum happy.

W&H: **What were the biggest challenges for you on the set?**

STW: I think the main challenge was the schedule, which was so tight, because we were pretty low budget. We were shooting what would normally be a three-day shoot in one day and we were almost shooting gorilla style. I think that was one of the biggest challenges, just trying to achieve everything we needed to achieve.

W&H: **What did you learn about yourself from making this?**

STW: That I tend to take on great big challenges. I think I learned a lot about myself in terms of that, really.

W&H: **What advice would you have for other women who are pursuing directing?**

STW: Don't be intimidated and make yourself known.

W&H: **I keep reading about the elimination of the UK Film Council. Every movie I see that comes from Britain has the UK Film Council listed in it.**

STW: They played a big part in our film, they really did. It was a significant part of the budget and who knows whether we would have gotten that anywhere else. I think what was important about the UK Film Council was that they weren't money generating. They weren't looking at the projects in terms of business—it meant they could fund very esoteric and artistic films and fund new filmmakers—it gave people an opportunity to make films that weren't necessarily going to be box-office smashes, but would be beautiful or interesting. They funded challenging, interesting filmmakers. They gave them a start and that happened to many people. It's difficult to know whether something like that will be replaced by the government, but it's doubtful. These institutions are unique and they can do that, and when one is taken away, it's very sad.

W&H: **Only 7 percent of the top grossing films in the United States are directed by women. I know it's a little higher in Great Britain. Why do you think it's still such a difficult nut to crack?**

STW: It's so hard to answer because you don't want to think or feel
       that in any way your gender is of any issue to you as a film-
       maker. I'm a filmmaker with the same potential and talent as
       the next, but it seems to be an issue, especially when you think
       Kathryn Bigelow is the first woman to win an Oscar and it is
       2010! I guess that makes it an issue—when you think, why is
       that? There is no answer . . .

Doris Yeung
Film Title: Motherland

Date of Release (or festival premiere): 2009 Outfest Film Festival

Link to IMDb Page: www.imdb.com/title/tt1331023

Link to Site: www.motherlandmovie.com

Link to Trailer: www.motherlandmovie.com

BIO: Doris Yeung was born in San Francisco in 1977 and raised in Hong Kong and California. She has written and directed films in China, Europe, and the United States, and graduated from the University of California, Los Angeles, and the Beijing Film Academy with degrees in art history and directing. She was also a Directing Fellow at the American Film Institute and has directed and written many experimental and narrative films including the short film *Dance*, which won the best short award at WorldFest Houston. Her films have played at the Director's Guild of America, San Francisco Museum of Modern Art, and numerous film festivals around the world. (*Motherland* official site)

DESCRIPTION: After a long absence abroad, a young Asian American woman, Raffi Tang, is called home when her estranged mother is murdered. She becomes increasingly drawn into a web of deception and incompetence while at the same time dealing with her own grief. The ultimate betrayal leads her to contorting truths in her family that have been hidden for far too long. Ultimately she learns that the American Dream can come at too high a price. (Credit: *Motherland* Official Website)

Interview Date: October 15, 2009

WOMEN AND HOLLYWOOD: What made you want to write and tell this story?

DORIS YEUNG: The story is inspired by my experience of grieving when my mother was murdered in 2004. I had been living in Europe (where I am still based) for a few years when I got a call to call home from a family friend who said they saw my house on television. I called my mother but there was no answer. Then I looked on the Internet on the *San Francisco Chronicle* and saw there was a murder in my hometown and then saw that it was my house and the victim was my mother. I returned to the United States for one year to deal with the police and lawyers. I was very frustrated with what I perceived as the lack of motivation and experience of the police on the case, which still remains unsolved. I have a filmmaking background, and decided to make a film as part of the grieving process and to draw more publicity to the case in the Bay Area. The film has not played in San Francisco yet but I hope to bring it there soon.

W&H: **You say that the film shows the destruction of the "American Dream." Can you elaborate on that?**

DY: I feel there are a lot of films, television, and media pieces which portray a one-sided vision of the "American Dream" as one of opportunity, where wealth and success are to be found for the hard-working and bold. It's a myth that is sold to countless immigrants and would-be immigrants to "lure" them to the country, to work in crappy jobs for their eventual piece of the dream.

What isn't mentioned is the dark side of the dream. What happens should one falter or perhaps fail? I'm interested in showing what happens to an immigrant family that appears to have achieved all the trappings of the dream, but, as a consequence, loses the actual family. In America, we place a lot of faith in justice, truth, and the American Way. We place faith in the institutions that are supposed to safeguard those concepts, but what I explore is what happens when those guardians fail, what can and should one do.

W&H: **Now that the film has played at Outfest, what are the next steps to get it seen by more people?**

DY: It is going around the festival circuit at the moment and we are looking for distributors. We are also looking at self-distribution opportunities.

W&H: **As a female director based in Europe, do you feel you have more opportunities as a woman director?**

DY: I do feel that as a female director in Europe, I have more opportunities due to the funding structure for the arts here. A lot of films are subsidized by the government that sometimes support minority and female artists so their voices can be heard. As filmmaking is a male-dominated industry, those grants are necessary to spur more women to make films if they have financial support. In fact we have just received a grant for my second film!

W&H: **What lessons and wisdom can you share with other women who want to be writers and directors?**

DY: The biggest lesson in being a film writer/director I learned is that if you want something, and you keep at it, come hell or high-water, you will achieve it.

DOCUMENTARIES

Photo Credit: Emily Abt

Emily Abt

DOCUMENTARY TITLE: *All of Us*

Date of Release (or festival premiere): 2008 Cleveland
International Film Festival

Link to IMDb Page: www.imdb.com/title/tt0826579

Link to Site: http://purelandpictures.com/All_of_Us_Home.html

Link to Trailer: http://purelandpictures.com/All_of_Us_Home.html

BIO: Selected as one of *Variety*'s "2009 Top 10 Directors to Watch," as well as *Paper* magazine's "Unhollywood 10 to Watch," Emily Abt is an award-winning filmmaker dedicated to creating both fiction and documentary projects. She is also the president of Pureland Pictures, Inc., a Brooklyn-based production company that she founded in 2000.

Abt's first film, *Take It From Me*, is a documentary about the human impact of welfare reform that she created when she was a caseworker in New York City. *All of Us*, her second documentary feature, was about a young doctor's fight against HIV/AIDS among black women. Abt's first narrative feature *Toe to Toe*, which she wrote, directed, and co-produced, premiered at the 2009 Sundance Film Festival and was released by Strand.

During her thirteen-year career as an independent filmmaker, Abt has also worked as a commercial director for clients such as Johnson & Johnson, Bloomingdales, Pfizer, MTV News & Docs, and many others. A graduate of Columbia University's MFA film program, Abt teaches Social-Issue Filmmaking at Princeton University and her current projects include her own script, *Audrey's Run*, about a woman who aspires to be the mayor of Boston, and *Buddy for Life*, a feature being produced by Circle of Confusion, which she is attached to direct. She produced an episode of *Love/Lust*, a television documentary on the Sundance Channel in 2011.

DESCRIPTION: In the South Bronx, a young doctor embarks on a research project to find out why black women are being infected with the HIV virus at an alarming rate. Dr. Mehret Mandefro takes us into the lives and relationships of two of her female patients, Chevelle and Tara, as they identify and struggle with the social factors that put them at risk. (Credit: *All of Us* Official Website)

Interview Date: September 18, 2008

WOMEN AND HOLLYWOOD: How did you meet Mehret and why did you want to tell this story?

EMILY ABT: I met Mehret Mandefro in 2003 when we were both
Fulbright Scholars in London. She was getting her master's
degree in public health of developing countries at the London
School of Hygiene and Tropical Medicine, and I was making
my Columbia University MFA thesis film about local Muslim
girls. We were both deeply committed to social change—she
as a doctor and me as a filmmaker—and wanted to know
more about why black women were being disproportionately
impacted by HIV.

Most effective social-issue documentaries start with an important question and that was ours. Black women are twenty-three
times more likely than white women to get HIV, and HIV is
still the leading cause of death for black women ages eighteen
to thirty-five. Mehret and I felt this reality was unacceptable
and wanted to turn a spotlight on the issue.

When I first began the film five years ago, I hoped there would
be a great deal of media coverage on the topic of HIV and black
women in America, as well as a good deal of public outrage
about the lack of funding allotted to deal with this health
crisis. But unlike the AIDS movement of the 1980s, largely
spearheaded by gay men, there has been no such movement on
behalf of the countless American black women who have suffered disproportionately from this disease.

W&H: **Please explain what ABC is and why it is not enough, especially
       for poor, urban, heterosexual women?**

EA: The "Abstain, Be faithful, use Condoms" approach to HIV
       prevention as endorsed by the George W. Bush administra-
       tion is irrelevant for the majority of women and young people,
       leaving them without the necessary information or tools they
       need to protect themselves. More specifically, ABC isn't effec-
       tive because it's been proven that abstinence-only education

does little to reduce sexual activity; marriage is actually a risk factor for HIV so the "be faithful" message misses the point. Using condoms is of course important but fails to take into account that women tend not to protect themselves when they're sleeping with men who have the upper hand, financially or otherwise. Public health experts on the ground must be able to determine the best mix of prevention programming that responds to the circumstances of the epidemic where they are working. As it stands, their hands are tied by mandates from Washington. Congress can and should change this.

W&H: **How did you find Chevelle and Tara, and also how did you get them to agree to have such intimate details and histories included in this film?**

EA: Chevelle and Tara were women that Mehret met through her work at Montefiore Hospital in the Bronx where she was doing her residency. It wasn't actually very difficult to get them to share their stories—they really wanted their voices to be heard.

W&H: **I was shocked when Mehret revealed that while she preaches safe sex to all her patients, she herself has not always practiced safe sex. What did that moment reveal about women and power in sexual relationships?**

EA: That moment showed that all women need to do a better job at being self-protective. When it comes to sexual health, progressives and feminists must push hard for change on a legislative level but also can't overlook promoting it on a personal level, as well. While the paternalistic protectionism of early years was clearly a destructive force for women, we must embrace a new self-protectiveness when it comes to our behavior in the bedroom and within our intimate relationships. I created *All of Us* to be used as a tool not only for social change, but also for personal change.

W&H: **How do we get the powers that be to take this epidemic more seriously?**

EA: Forgive me for being self-promotional, but suggesting they see *All of Us* isn't a terrible idea. Writing to our senators and insisting that they support Representative Barbara Lee's trailblazing Pathway bill is also a good start. And there needs to be a mass of people—whites, blacks, browns, men, women, etc.—all shouting that there's something wrong here. The message needs to come from all of us, because the advocacy groups aren't able to create enough public discourse on their own. And of course, vote for Obama.

W&H: **Explain the tag line—love and sex can mean life or death?**

EA: *All of Us* promotes the idea that when you're ready to have sex with someone, you should both get tested and share those results. Some people say, "Well, that's really awkward and not too romantic," to which I respond, "Should you really be sharing life's most intimate, sacred act with someone if you can't have that conversation?"

       As women, we have to start looking at the way we confuse love and sex. Men will happily sleep with a woman they don't love. It's one thing to be OK being that woman, and perhaps jeopardize yourself emotionally, but women are often also allowing themselves to be physically vulnerable in the scariest of ways. Women, across boundaries of race and class, are so hungry for love and intimacy from their male partners that they're willing to put their very lives on the line to get it. And when women contract HIV, or even a bad STD, they feel like damaged goods. They feel that their very worth as a human being has been lessened and can even become suicidal. So *All of Us* is trying to start some very crucial, life or death, conversations and asks viewers not just to watch this epidemic from a distance, but rather say to themselves, "There but for the grace of God, go I . . ."

W&H: **What are your goals for the film?**

EA: I hope *All of Us*, like all my films, inspires women to stand up for themselves. I'd like some teenager in the Bronx to see the film and say to herself, "You know, I'm not going to settle for casual sex when what I really want is a commitment." I'm hoping a college kid sees it and realizes there's no excuse for skipping the condom. I want the film to be used as a tool by the wonderful educators, social workers, medical health professionals, advocates, and the blessed community organizers that have made it their business to stop or slow this epidemic. And if I did my job right, then *All of Us* will spark dialogue and social change among thousands of women and girls who are unfortunately on the front-lines of great personal risk. If someone uses the film to advocate for a national sexual health plan (is it really OK that one in four teenage girls has an STD?) nothing would please me more. That's all, just a few modest goals.

W&H: **What did you learn from making this film?**

EA: I learned that sometimes making a film will leave you with battle scars, but that means you're battle-tested for the next one. And I learned (again) that art and politics can make a mighty fine combination if carefully mixed.

Photo Credit: Matthew Williams

Pietra Brettkelly

DOCUMENTARY TITLE:

The Art Star and the Sudanese Twins

Release Date (or festival premiere): 2008 Sundance Film Festival

Link to IMDb Page: www.imdb.com/title/tt1157607

Link to Site: www.theartstarandthesudanesetwins.com

Link to Trailer: www.theartstarandthesudanesetwins.com/trailer

BIO: Pietra Brettkelly describes herself as a passionate documentary maker. Her self-funded documentary *The Art Star and the Sudanese Twins* experienced international success at the Edinburgh International Film Festival, Hotdocs, Toronto, Zurich International Film Festival, the Melbourne International Film Festival, and Rio de Janeiro International Film Festival. The film won several awards, including Best Editing at Sundance and Best Documentary at Whistler Film Festival. She is the 2010 recipient of the New Zealand Film Commission Producer's Award.

In 2003 her film *Beauty Will Save the World* brought Brettkelly to Libya for the country's first beauty pageant, as well as an interview with then-colonel Muammar Ghadaffi. The film premiered at the American Film Institute Film Festival in Los Angeles. It had later screenings at Hot Docs, Toronto, and IDFA in Amsterdam. She produced and directed the television documentaries *Outward Bound* and *Maori Boy Genius* in 2011. (Credit: Pietra Brettkelly Website)

DESCRIPTION: *The Art Star and the Sudanese Twins* follows Vanessa Beecroft's intentions to adopt orphaned twins, Madit and Mongor Akot, and how this bleeds into her art and her personal life. For sixteen months, the film follows Vanessa with an often-brutal honesty, she exposes the truth about her life—her creative process, her struggle with depression, her volatile relationship with her husband, and her love for the twins. (Credit: *The Art Star and the Sudanese Twins* Official Website)

Interview Date: January 22, 2008

WOMEN AND HOLLYWOOD: **Even though Vanessa Beecroft is an internationally well-known artist, she is much better known outside the United States. Please introduce us to your subject.**

PIETRA BRETTKELLY: From what I understand, her persona as an artist is more well known in Europe because she was brought up in Italy. But she is one of the world's top contemporary artists, certainly one of the top female artists, and her focus has been tableaus of naked women that she stands in a room or space for three hours and people come and view them. Footage is taken of the tableau and those elements are sold as part of her artwork.

She's been doing this for thirteen years, and in the sixteen months that I was filming her, she was thinking about changing and adapting her work as an artist, as well. It seemed that things were coming to a head both personally and professionally in the time I was filming her.

W&H: **How did you come to pick Vanessa as the topic for your film?**

PB: I was in the Sudan filming another documentary and in southern Sudan there is an area where foreigners can rent a tent at night—it's mostly aide workers or NGOs. At night, you sit around a tree. Vanessa and her team were there; they didn't look like aide workers, and we started talking to them. When we were leaving, she said to me, "I'm thinking of adopting the twins [Madit and Mongor Akot] at the orphanage next door; I've been breastfeeding them during my last two visits to the Sudan." A couple of days later, I emailed her and said that international adoption is a topic that I've wanted to discuss and if she'd be interested I'd like to follow her story. I didn't even know she was an artist; I didn't even know what performance art was.

W&H: **It must have been hard as a director not knowing the direction your film was going to go in?**

PB: That's what I love about documentaries. It certainly was a curve ball when it gradually became obvious that her art was a very strong part of her and that she was famous. So then, I had to work out how much of that side of her needed to be part of the film and how I could incorporate it. I wasn't doing a profile of an artist. That was never my intention. My intention was to discuss international adoption. I did grapple with how much of her art needed to be in the film.

W&H: **Understanding her as an artist helps you understand her pursuit of these children.**

PB: The situation with many international adoptions is that there are parents and that's one of the aspects I wanted to discuss. They do have parents but it's through circumstances like poverty, war, or separation of some kind that they end up in orphanages or in situations where they don't have adult support. We think orphans have no parents but in developing countries, they often have parents.

W&H: **This brings up the issue of the fact that many women don't survive childbirth in these countries.**

PB: I was in Afghanistan on another film two-and-a-half years ago, and I went to this region where one out of five women dies in childbirth. Those numbers are horrific. That just shouldn't be happening and as the so-called privileged people, there is so much more we could be doing so these children wouldn't need to be adopted. I don't think it should be a given that our world is better than their world. One of the things I wanted to discuss was our future as a global community; if we want to create a situation in which, since we have the better world and the better life, we try to bring these children to our world.

W&H: **We realize very far into the film that Vanessa's husband [Greg Durkin] knows nothing about her intention of adopting the twins. Why didn't she tell him?**

PB: It's hard for me to say what she was thinking, because I would tend to think in a different way, as would you, so it's hard to figure out her motivation. She seemed to have convinced herself that she was researching the subject and then she would broach it with him and he would say, "Of course." I do think she was generally surprised that he wasn't interested in adopting the children. He's an intelligent person, socially and culturally sensitive, and he could appreciate that all children need an education and clean water, and these children didn't have those things. I think she thought that he would agree to it.

W&H: **She seems to be the type of person who gets her way a lot.**

PB: Yes.

W&H: **She thought she could probably convince him to do this, and she fell apart once she realized it wasn't going to happen. Talk about the scene where she has a breakdown after this realization.**

PB: We were shopping with her and she got a phone call, and we just wandered out onto the street and then she came out and we could see that she was crying. I'm like, "Oh my goodness"—that obviously was a phone call with Greg. You can see that initially we weren't focusing on her—we were just walking with her—and then I realized that she's OK with my filming this. I do have a conscience and some things aren't appropriate to film, but I knew that it was OK to film it. It was an incredible moment where she has this clarity that Greg is not going to agree to the adoption and that it isn't going to go forward. She was thinking, "Well, now how do I express my emotions?"—for her it was through her work.

W&H: **You are an active participant in the story, almost like a character behind the camera.**

PB: Those are the types of films I like to make, telling people's stories and following them through a particular or influential part of their lives. I'm not a great writer, but I'm good at asking questions. I'm fascinated by people, and those are the stories I want to tell. All my films are like that.

W&H: Vanessa says at the end, "I couldn't adopt the children I wanted to adopt so I had to do something." Is that what fueled the final scene at the Venice Biennale?

PB: The Biennale was an exploration of how she felt about the Sudan situation, about wanting to do something. She couldn't adopt the twins, so she looked for another way. One of the things that the film shows is that there is no line between Vanessa's art and her life and, therefore, the expression of her emotion for these twins is expressed in her art and the Biennale performance.

W&H: **What are you hoping people think about when they leave the theater?**

PB: I want them to discuss international adoption; to think about people from so-called privileged countries and how we should be helping people in developing countries. I don't think we can make a blanket statement about international adoptions being either right or wrong. I'd like people to appreciate that she is a complex character. She's different from anyone I've ever met, and this is a window to someone like that.

W&H: **We have many male performance artists who are more famous, and I was really shocked that I had no clue about the breadth of her work. She seems to be so controversial because her work is about women and women's bodies.**

PB: I know that she really struggles with her place as a woman in the art community, because there aren't many successful female artists in her field. She struggles with where she fits in. She was born in London, grew up in Italy, and then she immigrated to the United States. She's English and speaks with an Italian accent, yet in Italy they call her a British artist. Strangely, she feels really comfortable in the Sudan even though she has no connections to Africa. Finding herself has been a lifelong struggle for her.

Abby Epstein

DOCUMENTARY TITLE:

The Business of Being Born

Date of Release (or festival premiere): 2007 Tribeca Film Festival

Link to IMDb Page: www.imdb.com/title/tt0995061

Link to Site: www.thebusinessofbeingborn.com

Link to Trailer: www.thebusinessofbeingborn.com/trailer.php

BIO: Abby Epstein began her career in the theater. She was a theater director in Chicago and founded Roadworks Productions. In 1998, she became resident director of *Rent,* premiering the musical in Mexico City, Madrid, and Barcelona. Epstein made her directorial film debut with the documentary *Until the Violence Stops* at Sundance. It went on to screen on the Lifetime Network, receiving an Emmy. Her second documentary, *The Business of Being Born,* premiered at the Tribeca Film Festival, and she recently completed working on the film's sequel *More Business of Being Born.* She also co-wrote a book with producer, Ricki Lake, titled *Your Best Birth: Know All Your Options, Discover the Natural Choices, and Take Back the Birth Experience.*

DESCRIPTION: Birth is a miracle, a rite of passage, a natural part of life. But birth is also big business. Compelled to explore the subject after the delivery of her first child, actress Ricki Lake recruits filmmaker Abby Epstein to question the way American women have babies.

The film interlaces intimate birth stories with surprising historical, political, and scientific insights and shocking statistics about the current maternity care system. When director Epstein discovers she is pregnant during the making of the film, the journey becomes even more personal. (Credit: *The Business of Being Born* Official Website)

Interview Date: February 20, 2008

WOMEN AND HOLLYWOOD: How did you become involved with this film?

ABBY EPSTEIN: Ricki Lake and I became friends when I directed her in *The Vagina Monologues,* Off-Broadway. We stayed in touch, and I knew that she was planning a homebirth for her second child, which at the time I thought was completely nuts. A few years later, Ricki had finished her talk show and relocated to

Los Angeles so I stopped by to see her new house. I had just completed my first documentary, *Until the Violence Stops*, about the worldwide V-Day movement, and Ricki was looking to start a "dream" project about midwives and birthing. I was completely ignorant on the topic but intrigued by Ricki's passion, so I asked her for some reading material and she gave me a book called *Spiritual Midwifery*, by Ina May Gaskin. Then Ricki showed me the home video footage of her homebirth (which we use in the film), and I was completely blown away. We began from there.

W&H: **How did your involvement with the film affect your own birth experience?**

AE: On the one hand, I was very fortunate having spent two years researching birthing options in New York City before I became pregnant. I was a highly informed customer; I had attended several births and did not have any fear about the birth process. I felt I had all these amazing people to choose from when the time came to select a provider (of course, not all of them took my HMO insurance, so that limited me a bit). But on the other hand, I was put in a position where there was pressure to include my birth in the film—which I resisted. I had no interest in turning the cameras on myself and was unsure whether we were in fact going to document my birth until the very last moment.

W&H: **Explain why you chose the title *The Business of Being Born*.**

AE: Truthfully, we couldn't think of anything short and catchy. None of us really loved the title but it seemed to encompass the broad range of aspects we were looking at in the birthing "business."

W&H: **It seems that you and Ricki are both on a type of crusade here—using the film to help educate and organize women**

to take back their own bodies and their births. Did you ever
expect the film would morph into this type of movement?

AE: We never expected that the film would have such an impact on
        mainstream birth culture. I think we suspected that it would
        hit a nerve, but we honestly just wanted to put the information
        out there in a bold way—not water it down. It all stemmed
        from Ricki's personal experience and grew organically from
        there. But we have definitely started a movement along with
        other writers and activists—Jennifer Block's book *Pushed* was
        published at the same time we premiered, which was amazing.
        I think we are on a crusade to inform—but not to convince—
        women to have natural births or homebirths. The modern
        woman wants information and options—but no one should
        feel pressured or regretful about their choices.

W&H: There seems to be a lot of women directing documentaries
        these days. Why do you think that is?

AE: I think that documentaries often have more substance than
        features and women are attracted to material that is potent and
        meaningful rather than commercially viable. Of course, there
        is also the fact that docs are low budget and don't pay well (if at
        all!) so there is less competition.

        But mostly I think that docs are usually self-generated passion-
        projects, where a director can have total control (and women
        are organized, not afraid of hard work, and always like a bit of
        control).

W&H: What's next for you?

AE: We are still opening the film in major cities (Chicago, Seattle,
        Boston, Washington, D.C.), so I am busy with that until April.
        Ricki and I are in the midst of writing a book, based on the
        movie, which will come out in April 2009, and a follow-up

DVD that will accompany the book. We are also hard at work on our website, turning it into a resource for birth information and options. So, I will still be busy with things related to *The Business of Being Born* for a while and then I plan to direct an independent feature film. I'd like to get back to working with actors and writers, which is truly what I love.

Photo Credit: Beadie Finzi

Beadie Finzi

DOCUMENTARY TITLE: *Only When I Dance*

Date of Release (or festival premiere): 2009 Tribeca Film Festival

Link to IMDb Page: http://www.imdb.com/title/tt1393744

Link to Site: http://www.onlywhenidance.com

Link to Trailer: http://www.onlywhenidance.com

BIO: Beadie Finzi has been working in documentaries since 1994. After making a number of films for UK Broadcasters, Beadie produced *Unknown White Male*, a feature documentary about a young amnesiac rediscovering his life. Beadie went onto direct *The Hunger Season*, an emotional essay examining the impact of humanitarian food aid. In 2009, Beadie shot and directed *Only When I Dance*, which charts the remarkable story of two young children trying to dance their way out of the favelas of Rio. The film premiered at Tribeca Film Festival and was released in 2010 in the United Kingdom by Revolver and by Film Movement in the United States.

Beadie is one of the founding directors of the Channel 4 BRITDOC Foundation, a United Kingdom based not-for-profit organization dedicated to reinventing funding and distribution models for documentary filmmakers. It has funded more than award-winning films such as *Afghan Star, Yes Men Fix The World*, and the environmental polemic *The End of The Line*.

DESCRIPTION: *Only When I Dance* is a classic narrative documentary following two young teenagers, Isabela and Irlan, as they strive to realize an extraordinary dream. One girl, one boy; both black and poor, and living in one of the most violent favelas on the outskirts of Rio. Irlan and Isabela both want to dance—to dance ballet, and their ambition is to leave Brazil to join one of the great companies in the North. For them, dance is the way out, an escape, and on stage, an ecstasy that is rarely found in their day-to-day lives. The question is: Can they make it? *Only When I Dance* follows these two gifted teenagers during the year that will make or break all their future dreams. (Credit: *Only When I Dance* Official Press Materials)

Interview Date: July 2, 2010

WOMEN AND HOLLYWOOD: How did you find the subjects for the film?

BEADIE FINZI: Producers Giorgio Lo Savio and Christina Daniels were working up ideas and looking for possible characters, coming back and talking to me in London for nearly three years before we found Irlan and Isabella. There have been many competition style movies. Many extraordinary films are set in Rio de Janeiro. So it was a tall order to find something fresh and interesting, with deeper angles. Hence the numerous research trips and endless discussions over Caipirinhas before we identified just the right characters at the right time of their lives, who would also give us access.

W&H: Why did you think this would be a universal documentary?

BF: I really, really hoped it would be. The idea was always to make a cracking narrative film first, which had music and dance laced through. We wanted people who might never go and see classical or contemporary dance to watch the film and enjoy it. We hope that people may even be pleasantly surprised at how moving the dance could be.

W&H: Why did this story move you?

BF: There is a lot about this film that is emotional. However, for me the strongest themes were about family—about the love of good parents, of what they will do to give their children the very best chance. It was genuinely inspiring to be around Irlan's and Isabella's families. The selflessness, the good humor, in spite of the difficulties. It was a special year filming with them, and I must say I really miss them.

W&H: I found Isabella's story quite heartbreaking and Irlan's quite uplifting. How did you balance what was going on in both their lives?

BF: We only ever filmed those two and there was pressure at one stage to lose Isabella's story as Irlan's story began to take off. But for me there was no doubt they needed each other. It would have been too *saccharin* to have only featured Irlan. It would have looked too easy—"I had a dream, I wanted to dance. I danced my way out of the favela." What he has done is very extraordinary. It is the stuff of fiction, of dreams. But, the truth is most of us are like Isabella.

W&H: Isabella dealt with racism and body issues that were very difficult for her to conquer. Is the Brazilian ballet world much harder on girls?

BF: All schools of ballet are exacting on the body. There is a vision of the perfect body, of a grace of line, form, and proportions, which brings a huge pressure on all girls and women who participate in ballet. Brazil is no different in this, however, there are even greater issues here of race—the idea of wanting to be a black ballerina is preposterous. And coming from a poor background, well, it is laughable . . . and that is what makes Isabella such a hero and such an inspiration.

W&H: How did both their families' circumstances affect why these young people wanted to dance?

BF: It always seemed to me that dance was an escape from real life for Irlan and Isabella. Achieving moments of perfection, of discipline, and of beauty. A reprieve in one of the most intense, violent, and chaotic cities in the world.

W&H: What do you want people to get out of the film?

BF: I hope people are moved and inspired by Isabella and Irlan. These two make me feel anything is possible—dare to dream, dare to reach your dreams.

W&H: **What advice do you have for other female filmmakers?**

BF: Be ambitious in your filmmaking. Have persistence and quiet determination. But most of all, hold on to your passion for storytelling. Put aside all pressures in order to preserve authentic relationships and respect for your characters. I think that is totally essential.

W&H: **Tell us how you were able to get a distribution deal.**

BF: Producer Nikki Parrott of Tiger Lilly Films led the deal making. There was a fair amount of heat around this film—as a feel-good documentary that can work for quite a broad audience. Film Movement had come to see the film at Tribeca Film Festival and loved it, but then somehow in the craziness of the festival, our paths did not cross. They had assumed we were snapped up by others, so it was a delightful surprise when we reconnected at the end of last year and a struck a deal.

W&H: **What is next for you?**

BF: I am experimenting with a love story. Part musical, part documentary. Again with Nikki Parrott at Tiger Lilly. It's early, but I am excited!

Jennifer Fox

DOCUMENTARY TITLE:

Flying: Confessions of a Free Woman

Date of Release (or festival premiere): 2007 Sundance Film Festival

Link to IMDb Page: www.imdb.com/title/tt0846425

Link to Site: www.flyingconfessions.com

Link to Trailer: www.flyingconfessions.com/about_WatchTrailer.php

BIO: Jennifer Fox is an internationally acclaimed director, producer, camerawoman, and educator. Her first film, *Beirut: The Last Home Movie*, was broadcast in twenty countries, released theatrically in nine, and won seven international awards. She produced, directed, and shot the groundbreaking ten-hour series, *An American Love Story*, which aired in the United States nationally on PBS primetime.

She co-produced, directed, and shot the six-part film, *Flying: Confessions of a Free Woman*, through a Danish co-production. *Flying* premiered at the International Documentary Film Festival in Amsterdam (IDFA) in 2006 and the Sundance Film Festival in 2007.

Her current feature documentary, *My Reincarnation*, about a high Tibetan Master in exile and his Italian born son that was filmed over an unprecedented twenty years, was recently released.

DESCRIPTION: Never before in our collective human history have
so many women had such autonomy to construct a life of their own
creation. Yet, the terrain is still rocky and "choice" does not necessarily
bring happiness, let alone freedom. Meanwhile, old models of female-
ness still haunt women everywhere.

In this six-hour tour de force, *Flying: Confessions of a Free Woman*,
director Jennifer Fox lays bare her own turbulent life to penetrate what
it means to be a free woman today. As her drama of work and relationships unfolds over four years, our protagonist travels to more than
seventeen countries to understand how diverse women define their
lives when there is no map. Employing an ingenious new camera tech-
nique called "passing the camera," Fox creates a documentary language
that mirrors the special way women communicate. Over intimate
conversations around kitchen tables from South Africa to Russia, India
and Pakistan, she initiates a groundbreaking dialogue among women,
illuminating universal concerns across race, class, and nationality. Part
delectable soap opera, sociopolitical inquiry, and narrative experi-
ments, *Flying* sweeps us up into an addictive international adventure
chronicled with sincerity, innovation, and elegance. (Credit: *Flying:
Confessions of a Free Woman* Official Website)

Interview Date: May 12, 2008

WOMEN AND HOLLYWOOD: **Each episode starts off with the following resonant statement: "I never wanted to be a girl in the way
a girl was supposed to be. I wanted to be a boy. They could do
anything they wanted to do." Why was it important to begin
each episode that way?**

JENNIFER FOX: I think it really sums up the dilemma of our lives—
boys can do everything and girls can do very little. Remember,
I grew up in the late fifties but I have a feeling that girls grow

up not so different today . . . the gender lines have not been broken. And on this iconographic issue of raising children, in some ways, it's like we are back in the fifties.

W&H: **In the beginning episodes, you are focused on having a child after many years of ambivalence. You question whether you are a real woman in our culture without having a child.**

JF: We define women as being *married mothers* actually. It's marriage plus children.

W&H: **Do you feel you are in a different place from where you started the film?**

JF: You are looking at a woman who has run away screaming from a female identity, saying I will not be controlled by the rules, I will live as men live. At the beginning of the film, I am a long way from being a feminist because I completely sided with my father. I arrive at the end of the film siding with my mother and realizing that I am a part of a fabric that I didn't know I was part of before. At the end of the film [which was two years ago], I was still much more focused on having a child than I am now. I certainly feel that you can be woman and not have children, but I don't think society feels that.

W&H: **Do you think that if you had more of a feminist identity you would have come to the film from a different place?**

JF: Oh yeah, but I think the film would not have been as good. I think that if I had talked as politically as I do now, it wouldn't have made for a good film. What's good about the film is that I was in a crisis of identity; I couldn't speak the language because I couldn't identify. What you see is someone searching for who they are. That was real. The good news about the film is that you follow my journey and that made a better film, and one that younger women highly identify with.

W&H: Because you are not self-identified as a feminist?

JF: Right, and just like when I was a kid, a lot of people still see
       feminist as a bad word.

W&H: **Your film is heterosexually focused. Did you think about
       having lesbian stories as part of the film?**

JF: I did really want to have a lesbian story but all of my attempts
       failed. I always thought that at the end of the film I would
       break up with these two guys and go out with a woman as a
       way to investigate my bisexuality. It didn't happen. I think
       the problem is because there are so few films like this that we
       want it to cover everything. It's actually quite narrow. It's about
       sexual freedom and control. The main thing was that the film
       had be able to go around the world, not that it had to cover all
       female identities.

W&H: **What was so interesting was that you are taking people on
       a journey and exposing them to the international women's
       movement that many people here in the United States are so
       unfamiliar with.**

JF: I think what's really important about *Flying* is the issue of
       representation. We are used to looking at the third world in a
       kind of object-oriented way when the camera points at them
       and hides the filmmaker. What I was trying to do was to say
       that we in the United States who think we are so different
       from them are actually in the same frame. That's why it was
       so important for me to put a white, affluent, western woman
       in the same frame as a woman from Pakistan or Cambodia or
       India to visually shift the representation. I wanted to say these
       women are like us. That's why the issues of my sexual abuse
       and sexuality were so important to unravel in the film because
       they are so common and that totally breaks down the wall
       between us.

W&H: **Your film was financed internationally? How did you make that happen?**

JF: I have quite an international reputation in the documentary film scene. The reason why this was a Danish co-production is because of the filmmaking strategies—one person, one camera—and the intimacy is something they've done very successfully in Denmark. A producer approached me and we decided to partner. Doing a co-production is always quite hard. I lived in Denmark for a year and a half and my Danish editor was here and it's hard and always more expensive. In our case it was successful because there was a creative reason to work together.

W&H: **Why do you think that women are drawn to documentaries?**

JF: They are just so much fun to make and they are hands on. Politically—docs are more welcoming to women because of the smaller crews, smaller budgets, and less power—but at the same time it's also about having direct contact with a subject and people and I think women thrive on that. We are relationship beings.

       There are very few women making series, and when I made *American Love Story,* I was the only woman I knew in PBS land who made a series. I'm probably still the only woman to have directed and produced a ten-hour series for public TV. One of the issues I had to deal with (at the time) was how a thirty-something woman could be trusted with the scope and the money this would take. Those issues of money, power, and responsibility are always the same for women.

W&H: **Why do you think your film is resonating with people?**

JF: This film is resonating so differently because it generates profound dialogue. Women and men say to me: "This is my life

and nobody has put it on screen before, and it's such a relief."
I don't think that I've made a film that speaks so universally
and directly before. My films have been successful but this is
something different. Screening after screening I see this other
reaction. I see it as a movement. You have to let people talk.

W&H: **Do you embrace feminism now?**

JF: I do. A lot of the effort is to get people to talk about gender
        in a new way and to see that sexism and gender issues are so
        ingrained in us, and you have to do the daily work. It means
        don't capitulate to the idea of giving up your job because you
        have children. There is a point where we have to demand
        gender equality and you have to start with yourself.

Photo Credit: Robert G. Zuckerman

Roberta Grossman

DOCUMENTARY TITLE: *Blessed Is the Match:*
The Life and Death of Hannah Senesh

Date of Release (or festival premiere): 2008 San Francisco
Jewish Film Festival

Link to IMDb Page: www.imdb.com/title/tt0814031

Link to Site: www.blessedisthematch.com

Link to Trailer: www.blessedisthematch.com

DESCRIPTION: Narrated by Joan Allen, *Blessed Is the Match* is the first documentary feature about Hannah Senesh, the World War II-era poet and diarist who became a paratrooper, resistance fighter, and modern-day Joan of Arc.

Safe in Palestine in 1944, Hannah joined a mission to rescue Jews in her native Hungary. Shockingly, it was the only military rescue mission for Jews during the Holocaust. Hannah parachuted behind enemy lines, was captured, tortured, and ultimately executed by the Nazis. Incredibly, her mother Catherine witnessed the entire ordeal—first as a prisoner with Hannah and later as her advocate, braving the bombed-out streets of Budapest in a desperate attempt to save her daughter.

With unprecedented access to the Senesh family archive, and through interviews, eyewitness accounts, and the prolific writings of Hannah and

Catherine Senesh, *Blessed Is the Match* recreates Hannah's mission and imprisonment. The film explores Hannah's childhood against the backdrop of significant historical events, resulting in a rich portrait with several interlocking strands. (Credit: *Blessed Is the Match* Official Website)

Interview Date: January 28, 2009

WOMEN AND HOLLYWOOD: **What drew you to make this movie?**

ROBERTA GROSSMAN: I first read Hannah Senesh's diary when I was in junior high school and was really taken with her poetry and her passion, her writing and her high-minded idealism. I became a filmmaker right out of college and from that time I tried to make a film about Hannah Senesh. I was always writing proposals and grants and it never came together. It was for the best, because, by the time I was able to make the film, about three-and-a-half years ago, I was a mother and closer in age to Catherine Senesh—Hannah's mother—and I realized that the best way to tell this story was as a mother-daughter story. Heroic stories can be quite dull but the story of a mother watching her headstrong daughter do something that could take her life, and also of coming to rescue her—that was a potentially profound way to tell the story that would transcend ideas of heroism and would even transcend the Holocaust. Happily, Catherine Senesh published her diary, which I missed the first time around. She wrote a beautiful memoir about Hannah's childhood, the mission, and their time and that became the basis of the film. Catherine's memoir becomes the narration of the film, voiced by Joan Allen.

W&H: **How did you get Joan Allen involved?**

RG: I was just really lucky. It's six degrees of separation. I knew somebody who knew her lawyer, so we sent Joan the film, and she said yes. And she completely elevated the film. We worked with a scratch track for more than a year, and when Joan's voice was dropped into the film, it changed the film profoundly because she brought so much warmth and intelligence.

W&H: **Why did it take so long for a film about this woman to be made?**

RG: That's a really good question. I think that the family was very protective of Hannah's legacy and every time they had overtures from filmmakers and production companies, they didn't feel comfortable about turning over Hannah's story to that kind of exposure. It was the passage of time and the development of a relationship with me as someone they thought they could trust to tell the story.

W&H: **Did any of it have to do with the fact that most of the Holocaust stories are pretty much male—aside from Anne Frank?**

RG: There were a lot of women heroines in the resistance and there were two other women parachutists. I'm not a social historian so I can't answer why it took so long for a movie to be made about Hannah. All I know is that I am incredibly lucky that I ended up getting to be the person who made the film. I do think that generally (in the industry), women's stories are not the first to be told.

W&H: **I was struck by the scene of her coffin coming back to Israel and the reception she received.**

RG: That was a period of time (her body was returned in 1950), five years after the Holocaust and two years after the state of Israel was founded, when the country was new and young and desperately in need of inspirational stories. Hannah was held up as a symbol of resistance. She wasn't looked at as a young girl from Hungary who emigrated to Israel. She was held up as an Israeli heroine with that idea of Jews protecting themselves and fighting if necessary.

She was powerful beyond her actions. (Young women who go to the army are still taught about Hannah Senesh as a symbol of bravery.) Besides her actions, she left behind her diaries and her poems, so you could get an insight into the heart of the person. She was this warrior poet and that's a very powerful combination. In addition, her mother was there and Catherine became known in Israel as Mother Senesh, and she became a powerful figure in her own right. All these things together made it a perfect storm for Hannah becoming a national icon.

W&H: **Your film made it to the short list for the Academy Award.**

RG: I'm very grateful for that. I think the film is coming into its own now and people are beginning to hear about it. I hope people will see the film. I'm grateful that the process exists in such a way that a little movie that doesn't have buzz or a studio behind it can still be considered.

W&H: **Most documentaries have outreach campaigns for getting the word out. What are your goals beyond the theatrical release?**

RG: We started the outreach for the film almost at the same time we started making it. My feeling is that if you are going to make a film, you need to get it seen, and there are many avenues for getting a movie seen, and one of the most powerful is grass-roots outreach. We have a full-time director of outreach. Facing History and Ourselves, the leading Holocaust education organization, has been a partner for more than a year. We have created a thirty-two-page study guide and they are doing teacher training all across the country. We also created a forty-five-minute version of the film for junior high schools and high schools.

W&H: **Explain the importance of the title—*Blessed Is the Match*.**

RG: It is the title of the poem that Hannah wrote before she crossed
       the border into Hungary from Yugoslavia. She gave it to one of
       her fellow parachutists and asked him to bring it back to the
       Kibbutz if she didn't return. The poem is about self-sacrifice. A
       match is a very humble thing yet it can start a fire, and Hannah
       had the idea that one person could make a difference. I think
       it's remarkable that she had that sense of herself.

Photo Credit: Jacob Pritchard

Lisa F. Jackson

DOCUMENTARY TITLE:

The Greatest Silence:
Rape in the Congo

Date of Release (or festival premiere): 2008 Sundance Film Festival

Link to IMDb Page: www.imdb.com/title/tt1157650

Link to Site: http://thegreatestsilence.org

Link to Trailer: http://thegreatestsilence.org/about

BIO: Lisa F. Jackson has been making documentary films for more than thirty years, work that has brought her awards that include two Emmys and a Sundance Jury Prize. *Sex Crimes Unit*, her most recent film, is an unprecedented portrait of prosecutors in the Manhattan District Attorney's Office as they work to bring justice to victims of sexual violence. Jackson shot her last documentary in the war zones of the Democratic Republic of the Congo. The film exposes the horrifying fate of women and girls in an intractable war. It won a Special Jury Prize for Documentaries at the 2008 Sundance Film Festival, earned two Emmy nominations, and was broadcast on HBO.

For the last three years, Jackson has been shooting *Tres Mujeres (Three Women)*, a documentary about a group of displaced women living in the slums of Bogotá, Colombia. It is currently in post-production. She also serves as producer of the popular television show *Secret Millionaire*.

Jackson studied filmmaking at MIT with Richard Leacock and has directed and/ or edited dozens of films for PBS including *Voices and Visions: Emily Dickinson*; *Jackson Pollock: Portrait, Through Madness*. She has screened her work and lectured at the Columbia University School of Journalism, Brandeis, Purdue, New York University, Yale, Notre Dame, and Harvard University, and was a visiting professor of documentary film at the School for Visual Arts in Manhattan.

DESCRIPTION: Since 1998 a brutal war has been raging in the Democratic Republic of Congo (DRC). More than four million people have died. And there are the uncountable casualties: the many tens of thousands of women and girls who have been systematically kidnapped, raped, mutilated, and tortured by soldiers from both foreign militias and the Congolese army.

The world knows nothing of these women. Their stories have never been told. They suffer and die in silence. In *The Greatest Silence: Rape in the Congo*, these brave women finally speak. (Credit: *The Greatest Silence* Official Website)

Interview Date: January 24, 2008

WOMEN AND HOLLYWOOD: **Why did you want to make this movie?**

LISA JACKSON: It's an invisible story, as many of women's stories are,
the horrific tale of the systematic rape and mutilation of hundreds and thousands of women. It's just stunning to me that
nobody was reporting it. The *New York Times* did one story on
this angle of the war. But what they are doing to women . . . not
only the militias from the neighboring countries but also the
Congolese army itself. I interviewed soldiers who were raping
the very women they were supposed to be protecting.

W&H: **It was amazing that when you were talking to the rapists, they
had a complete and total disconnect from the harm they were
actually causing.**

LJ: The Congolese army see themselves as just "raping," whereas the
militias are the ones who mutilate the women and fire guns into
their vaginas. But the end result is exactly the same. The women
are shunned, turned out from their villages, and abandoned. The
end result is exactly the same and that they parse the difference
is just ridiculous. This disconnect is pretty profound.

W&H: **You made yourself a character in the film. Why did you do
that?**

LJ: It wasn't something I was initially going to do, but people
who saw rough cuts said that I absolutely had to because it
was through telling my story of being raped that the barriers
between us came down.

W&H: **What compelled you to go to the Congo?**

LJ: Here was this story—the stories of these women—and no one
was telling it. It seemed important to me not to have some
hand-wringing piece but to actually listen to these women's

stories. These are women who are silent and for them to be able to share their story with someone who was not judging them was an experience none had ever had.

I went to Kinshasa on frequent flyer miles and with documentaries, you never know what you are getting into. I don't have much experience shooting in conflict zones, but a friend working with the UN Peacekeepers was able to get me a UN credential. I then made my way east to where the real nightmare was unfolding.

My radar is particularly attuned to those voices, which are the other side of war. I thought for years of doing a survey film on the fate of women and girls in conflict zones because of the ongoing devastating effects of war. So I went to the worst place first to shoot.

I am continuing the theme and have been to Colombia twice in the last three months doing a film on displaced women. It is said that 60 percent of the women in Colombia have suffered either physical or sexual violence. This is another one of those invisible stories, and it is a requirement of a documentary to find stories that otherwise you would never hear about.

W&H: **How did it feel being a first-world white woman going into a third-world country?**

LJ: I thought that through before I went. I was a white woman in the bush with a camera. I might as well have been dumped from a spaceship. I thought that it was important to let them know I was one of them, as much as I could, so I brought photographs to demystify where I was coming from and I shared my story of rape. They kept asking me about the war, thinking that rape only occurs in time of war. They asked lots of questions including, "Did your family know you were raped" and "How was it you got married?" They were fascinated that I now had a boyfriend, and were stunned to hear that I chose not to have children.

Their questions pointed to how different we really were. I feel an intense responsibility to them. It was the rare woman who would tell her story without pleading for help for her and her sisters.

W&H: **Why do you think that women directors are so well represented in documentaries versus features?**

LJ: I've only made documentaries for thirty-five years, but the thing about docs, especially now, is that you have the option of doing it on your own. On this film, I directed, shot it, did the sound, and edited it—I was a one-person band. I tried for almost a year to get funding. I have never done a doc this way but you really do have that option, especially working on a small scale. You have a lot more control. This is also a film that nobody would have funded because it's such a bummer subject, but once people see it, they are shocked that nobody has done it before. I knew that once I got over there and started filming, that I would get support because people would see the women's faces, hear their stories, and then realize what a compelling subject it was.

W&H: **What can people do to help?**

LJ: We are putting together an outreach strategy around the culture of impunity to pressure the Congo government to prosecute rapists. We will provide resources where people can donate money. But also it's important for developed nations to look at its role. This is an economic war. The blood of Congolese women is on our cell phones. It's important to understand that it's not just a bunch of crazy Africans killing one another. There is an economic imperative behind the pillaging, killing, and rape.

To strike at the women is to strike at the heart of the culture. If you destroy women, the civilization collapses.

Photo Credit: Bruce Guthrie

Aviva Kempner

DOCUMENTARY TITLE: *Yoo-Hoo, Mrs. Goldberg*

Date of Release (or festival premiere): July 10, 2009

Link to IMDb Page: www.imdb.com/title/tt1334479

Link to Site: http://mollygoldbergfilm.org/home.php

Link to Trailer: http://mollygoldbergfilm.org/home.php

BIO: Washington, D.C., based filmmaker Aviva Kempner wrote, produced, and directed the critically acclaimed *Yoo-Hoo, Mrs. Goldberg*, and the Emmy-nominated and Peabody-awarded *The Life and Times of Hank Greenberg*. She produced and co-wrote the award-winning *Partisans of Vilna*. She is presently making a documentary about how Chicago philanthropist Julius Rosenwald partnered with Booker T. Washington in establishing more than five thousand schools for African Americans in the rural South. Kempner co-wrote and is co-producing the dramatic script *Navajo Nation*. She also founded the Washington Jewish Film Festival and has written film reviews for the past twenty-five years. She was the recipient of the 2009 San Francisco Jewish Film Festival's Freedom of Expression Award, a Guggenheim Fellowship, the D.C. Mayor's Art Award, and the Women of Vision Award and Media Arts Award from the National Foundation for Jewish Culture.

DESCRIPTION: From Aviva Kempner, maker of *The Life and Times of Hank Greenberg*, comes this humorous and eye-opening story of television pioneer Gertrude Berg. She was the creator, principal writer, and star of *The Goldbergs*, a popular radio show for seventeen years, which became television's very first character-driven domestic sitcom in 1949. Berg received the first Best Actress Emmy in history, and paved the way for women in the entertainment industry. The film includes interviews with Supreme Court Justice Ruth Bader Ginsburg, actor Ed Asner, producers Norman Lear (*All in the Family*) and Gary David Goldberg (*Family Ties*), and NPR correspondent Susan Stamberg. (Credit: *Yoo-Hoo, Mrs. Goldberg* Official Press Materials)

Interview Date: July 10, 2009

WOMEN AND HOLLYWOOD: **Why did you want to tell Gertrude
Berg's story?**

AVIVA KEMPNER: For the past thirty years, I have done films about
Jewish heroes—men and women who fought the Nazis, and
baseball slugger Hank Greenberg. This time I wanted to con-
centrate on a heroine who had such a positive influence on
American culture.

W&H: **Gertrude accomplished so many things in her life and was
truly famous in her time, yet she is completely unknown
especially to younger audiences. How did she get to be "the
most famous woman in America you've never heard of"?**

AK: Her shows were not syndicated, she suffered co-star Philip
Loeb's blacklisting, and she was on TV so long ago that she is
not duly remembered.

W&H: **Gertrude was in charge of all facets of her show from writing
to producing to casting—everything. What lessons can we
take from Gertrude for today?**

AK: Use every minute of the day. She would write from six to
nine in the morning, then her husband Lewis would type her
scripts. Then she would go to the studio and produce, and then,
without much effort, slide into her role as Molly Goldberg.

W&H: **Why have you made it your life's work to make documentaries about under-known Jews?**

AK: As a child of a Holocaust survivor who lost three grandparents
and an aunt to the Holocaust, I consider it my life's mission to
make films about Jewish heroes and heroines that contradict
negative stereotypes about Jews.

W&H: Gertrude was so big and important in the industry that she was able to fend off the "blacklist" for some time and protect her lead actor Philip Loeb. Yet she could not hold it off forever, and was eventually forced to remove Loeb, which caused the show and her career to suffer. Can you talk about what it meant for a woman to do what she did at that time?

AK: I think any man or woman at that time was heroic to stand up to the blacklist, and it makes me proud that one of the most courageous stories came from a Jewish woman.

W&H: **What is the favorite thing you discovered about Gertrude Berg?**

AK: She wrote in the bathtub every morning at six. Now I wake up that early to work.

W&H: **You really want younger women to learn about Gertrude. Why is that so important to you?**

AK: Our tagline is "the most famous woman in America you never heard of" and that alone makes it an important film for younger women to see. Also, we want Americans to know that the first inspiration for the domestic sitcom was Berg, and that you can be funny and poignant without having to be gross or over the top.

W&H: **What story are you thinking of working on next?**

AK: I co-wrote a dramatic script about a Navajo activist that I want to produce, as well as documentaries on labor leader Samuel Gompers and the establishment of the Rosenwald schools.

Photo Credit: Ethan Kaplan

Lynn Hershman Leeson

DOCUMENTARY TITLE:

!War Women Art Revolution

Date of Release (or festival premiere): 2010 Toronto International
    Film Festival

Link to IMDb Page: www.imdb.com/title/tt1699720

Link to Site: www.womenartrevolution.com

Link to Trailer: www.womenartrevolution.com

BIO: Lynn Hershman Leeson's first feature film, *Conceiving Ada*, was shown at the 1998 Sundance Film Festival, the Toronto International Film Festival, the Berlin International Film Festival, and thirty-five other festivals worldwide. It received the Outstanding Achievement in Drama Award from the Festival of Electronic Cinema (Chiba, Japan, 1999), and it was nominated for an Independent Spirit Award (1999). Her second feature film, *Teknolust*, premiered at festivals in Toronto and Berlin, as well as Sundance. Hershman Leeson's direction and screenplay for *Teknolust* were recognized with the Alfred P. Sloan Foundation Feature Film Prize in Science and Technology (2003).

Hershman received a John Simon Guggenheim Memorial Foundation Fellowship, which supported *!War Women Art Revolution*. The film was released by Zeitgeist Films and featured at the Toronto, Sundance, and Berlin International Film Festivals.

Leeson's artwork has been exhibited at more than two hundred major art institutions, including the Museum of Modern Art and The National Gallery of Canada. She is chair of the Film Department at the San Francisco Art Institute and Professor Emeritus at the University of California.

DESCRIPTION: *!War Women Art Revolution* elaborates the relationship of the feminist art movement to the 1960s anti-war and civil rights movements and explains how historical events, such as the all-male protest exhibition against the invasion of Cambodia, sparked the first of many feminist actions against major cultural institutions. The film details major developments in women's art of the 1970s, including the first feminist art education programs, political organizations and protests, alternative art spaces such as the A.I.R. Gallery and Franklin Furnace in New York and the Los Angeles Women's Building, publications such as *Chrysalis and Heresies*, and landmark exhibitions, performance, and installations of public art that changed the entire direction of art.

New ways of thinking about the complexities of gender, race, class, and sexuality evolved. The Guerrilla Girls emerged as the conscience of the art world and held academic institutions, galleries, and museums accountable for discrimination practices. Over time, the tenacity and courage of these pioneering women artists resulted in what many historians now feel is the most significant art movement of the late twentieth century. (Credit: *!War Women Art Revolution* Official Website)

Interview Date: September 13, 2010

WOMEN AND HOLLYWOOD: This is the most feminist film I have seen in a very long time. Was that your intention?

LYNN HERSHMAN LEESON: I was trying to tell the story. When people started talking to me in the late 1960s, the feminist art movement wasn't even named. We were just trying to find a voice. My hope is that this tells a story nobody knows, and I hope it inspires people to have courage to be fearless in their convictions and to put into the world the things they need to say.

W&H: **How has women's art evolved during the last forty years?**

LHL: Feminist art moved into the art world through men, although they may not know it. If you take works by Matthew Barney or Matthew Kelly, they really use a lot of the theories and ideas of the feminist movement in their work. The work has evolved to the point where it is just beginning to be recognized, especially with the WAC show just a few years ago. Now 30 percent of curators at the Museum of Modern Art are women, and they are young, and that will make a terrific difference in the kind of shows that are going to happen there.

W&H: **How did the women artists get along with some of the "mainstream" feminist thinkers of the time?**

LHL: There were a lot of factions and much exclusion. Things happened in pockets that were not linear or cohesive. People would get certain moments of support within the community but it didn't really have a broad reach because there was no communication system like there is today.

W&H: **Some of the artists felt disappointed that their personal work didn't have as broad an impact as they had hoped. Was that your impression?**

LHL: It's interesting because certain artists who do have a broad impact and are well known around the world don't realize it. They still operate under the illusion that they are not effective and are invisible.

W&H: **Why do you think that is?**

LHL: I think because they are so used to it. It's almost like they are brainwashed into believing that nobody knows who they are. One very famous artist was surprised that students knew who she was. I think it is going to take another generation for artists to have the confidence of knowing that what they are doing is having an impact.

W&H: **What would success mean for you in terms of how this film gets out into the world?**

LHL: I really want people to see it. I'd love to have it on TV, have it theatrically distributed, have the DVD available, and to have it broadly seen educationally and in museums. I think this is a critical part of American history that has consciously—or not—been left out of history. It's a vital tool for inspiring other people on how to deal with exclusion and to use their creative voice in a way that has an impact.

W&H: **There's a line in the movie that says, "The personal became political and the very personal became art." Can you elaborate on that?**

LHL: One of the most popular sayings of the feminist movement is
       that the personal is political. How people act in the world, with
       their family, is political. The deeper you go into your truth and
       your own personal history and address those issues, the more
       people you are going to reach. It takes courage to do that.

W&H: **Talk a little about where the title** *!Women Art Revolution*
       came from.

LHL: That was actually the first group that formed in the late
       1960s. People would mention it but nobody knew anything
       about it. In fact, I just got an email last week from one of
       women who founded it. I wish I would have known about
       her two years ago. It seemed appropriate to start with that.
       Also, the ideas of the wars—not just the ones fought for to
       have a voice, but also the wars that one fights in Congress
       to overturn a bill, as well as the wars in Cambodia and
       Vietnam. There has been a succession of wars and landmines
       in order to accomplish this goal.

W&H: **It took you forty years to make this film. Explain why you**
       needed so long to put this together.

LHL: I felt like there was never an ending to the struggle. After
       the WAC show, things started to change and there were
       enlightened women philanthropists putting their money into
       museums and insisting on women's exhibitions. And they
       also bought women's art. You saw that last year at MOMA,
       the Pompidou, and the Tate. I also feel that the technology is
       now at a point where I can, for example, put all the footage
       online. We have another site called RAW/WAR that we will
       launch at Sundance, which will allow future stories to be
       added to the archive. All these things coalesced at this time.

W&H: **Do you feel that the feminist art movement is as relevant now?**

LHL: I think it is. I think that younger women need to know what a struggle it was to have the access they now have, even though it is still not equal access. I think there is a continual reinvigoration of one's values in culture.

W&H: **What do you want people to think about when they leave the theater?**

LHL: I want them to understand that it wasn't easy, that it wasn't a given—that people had to overturn many obstacles in order to create something that the next generation can move forward from. And also that there is value to what one does—whether or not it is acknowledged in one's own lifetime. That one has the option of living with courage and fearlessly surviving with dignity and doing the thing that only they can do.

W&H: **What advice do you have for other women filmmakers?**

LHL: Stay with your own truth, keep your sense of humor, and don't give up.

Photo Credit: Greg Kessler

Photo Credit: Abigail Disney

Gini Reticker (DIRECTOR)
Abigail Disney (PRODUCER)

DOCUMENTARY TITLE:

Pray the Devil Back to Hell

Date of Release (or festival premiere): 2008 Tribeca Film Festival

Link to IMDb Page: www.imdb.com/title/tt1202203

Link to Site: www.praythedevilbacktohell.com/v3

Link to Trailer: http://praythedevilbacktohell.com/video-media.php

BIOS: Gini Reticker is one of the world's leading documentary filmmakers whose primary focus is on individuals, particularly women, engaged in struggles for social justice and human rights. Her filmmaking has taken her to conflict zones around the globe, including Liberia, Rwanda, and Afghanistan. Reticker is the executive producer of PBS's series *Women, War & Peace*. Her earlier work includes the 2004 Academy-Award-nominated short *Asylum*. She was also the producer/co-director of *Heart of the Matter*, *Ladies First*, and *The Class of 2006*, amongst several others. (Credit: *Pray the Devil Back to Hell* Official Website)

Abigail E. Disney is a filmmaker, philanthropist, and scholar. She has produced a number of documentaries focused on social themes, including the award-winning 2008 film *Pray the Devil Back to Hell*, which discovered and shared with the world the little-known story of how a small band of women dared to break barriers of gender and politics in Liberia and end a century of entrenched civil war. The film inspired her to form Peace is Loud (peaceisloud.org), an organization that supports female voices and international peace building through nonviolent means. Her film, *Women, War & Peace* recently aired on PBS.

DESCRIPTION: *Pray the Devil Back to Hell* chronicles the remarkable story of the courageous Liberian women who came together to end a bloody civil war and bring peace to their shattered country.

Thousands of women—ordinary mothers, grandmothers, aunts, and daughters, both Christian and Muslim—came together to pray for peace and then staged a silent protest outside the Presidential Palace. Armed only with white T-shirts and the courage of their convictions, they demanded a resolution to the country's civil war. Their actions were a critical element in bringing about an agreement during the stalled peace talks.

A story of sacrifice, unity, and transcendence, *Pray the Devil Back to Hell* honors the strength and perseverance of the women of Liberia.

Inspiring, uplifting, and most of all motivating, it is a compelling testimony of how grass-roots activism can alter the history of nations. (Credit: *Pray the Devil Back to Hell* Official Website)

Interview Date: May 2, 2008

WOMEN AND HOLLYWOOD: You and Gini seem to have a real collaborative relationship beyond the typical producer/ director.

ABBY DISNEY: Gini trusts me a lot and vice versa.

W&H: How did this movie come about?

GINI RETICKER: Abby and I hadn't seen each other for years and we ran into each just after Abby had been to Liberia. We were totally on the same page about what was important in the story. It was wonderful to have her and she was also respectful of me in the edit room. She would make suggestions that respected my experience. It's been an incredibly dynamic relationship.

W&H: Talk about the title.

GR: One of the main characters in the film, Leymah Gbowee, says that [former President] Charles Taylor could pray the devil out of hell and it was such a great expression. That's what the women did by banding together—they prayed the devil back to hell. I don't think that it was only Charles Taylor as the man, but it was the evil force they saw. The country had lost its moral compass and the women came forward and said, "Hey, let's get this under control."

W&H: Abby, you financed the film yourself?

AD: Yes, it seemed easier rather than having to go to people and ask for money. It gave me nimbleness and an ability to react more quickly and to think independently without having to answer to anybody.

W&H: **What was the budget?**

AD: We spent around $800,000. It was not an easy shoot. There is
no power in Liberia so you need generators. We had to build
our own sets and I was not about to go without insurance.
As the producer, I felt very responsible for everyone and their
safety. And Gini is well respected, as is Kirsten Johnson—the
director of photography—and these are people who should be
paid appropriately.

W&H: **Talk a bit about what you've learned from your first foray into
the movie business.**

AD: I didn't have a lot of the problems women have because I didn't
need to go and ask for money. I didn't have to talk to anyone
in charge of the purse strings and convince them as to why
this was important because I knew this was a tough sell. Even
if there are women in charge they are still accountable to men.
So they are very averse to taking risks especially if it's seen as a
"women's thing." It's difficult to get anybody in the mainstream
media to understand this. That's why I felt I was uniquely posi-
tioned to get this done.

W&H: **Can you talk about working as a woman director and any difficulties you have faced.**

GR: For me, working in documentaries has been really easy and
it's manageable with having a family, which has been really
nice because I had some control over my career. I've always
been drawn to women's issues. Before I made documentaries, I
worked in women's health care and that is what drew me to my
first film. I think that working in documentaries has been the
ideal profession for me.

W&H: **You've been involved in women's issues for a long time but
never felt compelled to tell a story before.**

AD: I've felt compelled to tell a story before just not compelled enough to do it.

W&H: **Why was this different?**

AD: Everything lined up on this one. Part of it is how old my children are and how much time I had. This really was a story that was going to be erased from the historical records that was really worth holding onto.

W&H: **Talk more about how women's accomplishments get erased from history.**

AD: Yesterday I was talking to a high school class after a screening and asked them if they heard of Sacagawea and of course they had. They had, because there were women who worked and resurfaced the memory of her. She was not in the historical records when I was in high school. The persistent manner we have defined as authority excludes women—if they don't look authoritative they don't get captured in the media and then don't get converted into the historical record. We clearly knew what was going on in Liberia. The news media didn't look at what the women were doing as authoritative, so they simply did not point their cameras in that direction. We had no problems finding the footage of the killing, the shooting, and the maiming, but when the women were working for peace the cameras were not pointed in that direction. That tells us a great deal about what the news media thinks is worth telling and how much of what genuinely happens do we get to hear.

W&H: **You mentioned before that we tend to see women in Africa as victims, not through their accomplishments, and that it was an important for you to tell this positive story.**

GR: Most of the media you see on Africa portrays Africa and Africans as victims and not agents of their own lives. I feel that the people that I met there are just like you and me. As a documentary filmmaker, I am always drawn to what I have in common with someone rather than that which makes us different. The common bond of humanity is fascinating and so I was hell bent on making sure the women were able to tell their own story and were portrayed in the way I saw them. That way it is much easier to be inspired by them.

W&H: **Our country is not aware of the global women's movement, and you have an opportunity to bring international feminist issues to this country.**

AD: I don't think it will be hard. I tell people how the women in Kurdistan and Georgia wept and then wrote a peace agenda when they saw the film. I think this will be very appealing to women if we get it to them through the right medium, through the right messenger, and in the right form.

W&H: **Can you please explain?**

AD: We are going to work on finding the right messengers on TV, radio, and the Internet to bring this message to women.

W&H: **How are you going to get the film out there? Do you have a distributor?**

AD: I'm not going to a distributor with my hat in my hand begging them to distribute the film. If we don't get a good deal, we will distribute it ourselves.

W&H: **Hollywood doesn't seem to be interested in women's stories. What are your feelings about that?**

GR: I think it's a case of blindness to a real market, to a real hunger. That's the response we are getting from this film. There is a hunger for stories that are more hopeful, that show a different side of things. The distribution of this film will be fascinating.

We will try to have a theatrical release, but we are getting requests from people who want to fill movie theaters around the country. We're getting more requests to show the film than we can deal with at this time. We are trying to harness all that and also look at alternative distribution models, but I think we will probably do a hybrid and do everything. I would have to say hats off to Abby because she has enormous aspirations and energy and she is really committed to this film and to the ideas behind it.

W&H: **And you will create a curriculum and other educational devices?**

AD: The opportunities are vast—through educational institutions, religious institutions, girls clubs, youth organizations, and women's organizations—and there is a curriculum for each one of these groups.

W&H: **Many times people say movies are just movies, and that they don't have the power to make change and to affect people.**

AD: Movies are just movies if that's how you go about making them. Of all the media we have, this is the closest in tone and feeling to the dream that comes from the deepest part of ourselves. We do such a disservice to ourselves by not using this medium with the respect it deserves, because it innately has enormous power to address our deepest needs values and longings. That's why my uncle (Walt Disney) was very good at what he did. He understood that film had enormous power—to go right into the center of who a person was. That's why I wanted to make this film. I couldn't write this as a book and I couldn't go around the world and tell people the story. You needed to have everything come together in music and visuals and sound in the way it does in this film, and I think Gini has done an effective job in making sure that the whole thing coheres.

W&H: **What would your uncle say about this film?**

AD: I'm not sure. I know he was a man of his time in many ways, politically he was very conservative and he was afraid of communists. But I also know he had a good heart, and I don't think this film is about politics—it appeals to people, without politics. Sometimes you need to strip away the politics and restore the dialogue. I think he'd love it, in that way.

W&H: **What do you want people who see this film to get out of it?**

GR: The response so far has been tremendous. It has exceeded my expectations. I feel that people are being inspired in all sorts of different ways that I could never have imagined. There are people who see this as instrumental to doing peace work. I woke up yesterday morning to an email from women in Tbilisi, Georgia, saying that they had seen the film and had shown it to other women. Their region is having heightened militarism with ethnic overtones and they decided to take up the mantle of the women of Liberia and are starting their own peace movement. What could be better than that! Women in Sudan say it's going to change their lives. On that level, it's beyond my wildest hopes.

W&H: **What are you doing next?**

GR: Abby and I are continuing to work together and are co-producing a four-hour series on women in conflict for Wide Angle on PBS titled *Women, War and Peace* (www.pbs.org/wnet/wideangle/).

Hannah Rothschild

Date of Release (or festival premiere): November 25, 2009 (HBO)

Link to IMDb Page: www.imdb.com/title/tt1337112

Link to Site: www.thejazzbaroness.com

Link to Trailer: www.hbo.com/documentaries/the-jazz-baroness/video/trailer

BIO: Hannah Rothschild is a writer and director. Her documentary features have appeared on the BBC, HBO, and at film festivals, including Telluride, the London Film Festival, and Sheffield. She has directed, produced, and filmed *The Jazz Baroness, Hi Society*, and *Mandleson: The Real PM*. Working Title and Ridley Scott optioned her original screenplays. Her features and interviews appear in newspapers and magazines, including *W, Vanity Fair, The Telegraph, The Times, The New York Times, The Spectator*, British and American *Vogue*. (Credit: *The Jazz Baroness* Official Website)

DESCRIPTION: *The Jazz Baroness* tells the moving love story of Pannonica Rothschild ("Nica" for short) and pianist-composer Thelonious Monk. Directed by Nica's great-niece Hannah Rothschild, the documentary features the voice of Oscar® winner Helen Mirren, who reads Nica's words.

From wildly different beginnings—his on a humble farm in the American Deep South, hers in luxurious European mansions frequented by kings, queens, and heads of state—the film traces their lives up to the point of meeting, then follows their time together in a post-World War II New York City buzzing with pre-civil rights tension and the frenetic syncopation of bebop. Rothschild's film profiles an extraordinary woman who devoted herself to the cause of New York's jazz elite, who were not only struggling artistically, but battling a racist culture. (Credit: *The Jazz Baroness* HBO Website)

Interview Date: November 24, 2009

WOMEN AND HOLLYWOOD: **Why do you think that this unique relationship between Nica and Thelonious Monk has gone virtually unreported until now?**

HANNAH ROTHSCHILD: At the time they were hanging out, in the 1950s, '60s, and '70s, everyone on the scene knew because they saw them out together. But it's been twenty-one years since she died and twenty-seven since he did. Interest in their relationship, and in Nica in particular, was reignited when her children and granddaughter Nadine published Nica's book *Three Wishes* posthumously. It's a wonderful journal of her personal photographs and her interviews with musicians where she asked them, if they had three wishes what they'd be. After that, lots of people's memories and interest were tweaked.

W&H: **What made you need to tell this story?**

HR: I was lucky enough to know Nica and, since I worked as a
       documentarian, I wanted to find out more about this relative.
       Her story reflected so many things I am interested in—history,
       women, music, human rights, America, Europe, and my
       family. It seemed like a gift.

W&H: **Clearly Nica was a woman ahead of her time in many differ-
       ent ways. What can we learn from her sense of independence
       and passion?**

HR: She was born in 1913, at a time when women didn't have
       the right to vote and, in most cases, did not have access to
       education or employment except as domestic servants. Her
       youth was a waiting room for motherhood and marriage. In
       the United Kingdom, until the divorce act of 1969, women
       weren't granted either alimony or custody of their children.
       The only two groups banned from private enclosures at race-
       courses, for example, were convicted felons and divorcees.
       Against this backdrop, her decision to cross continents and
       fight for the rights of a group of people whom she considered
       badly treated serves as an inspiration. She was an early femi-
       nist and freedom fighter.

W&H: **I found it so interesting that Nica seems to have been virtually
       erased from the Rothschild legacy. How painful is that for you
       and why do you believe that occurred?**

HR: I hope that from now on she will be fully reinstated. In our
       family, until now, women have, with notable exceptions, been
       erased from the records. Only the children of the eldest sons
       are included in the family tree: my daughters for example don't
       merit an entry because their mother is not the heir. I don't find
       it "painful," it's just weird.

W&H: **What was the most important thing you learned about your-self and Nica from making the film?**

HR: To put principles before personalities, to stand up for what you believe in, but also accept that others are entitled to their opinions.

W&H: **What advice do you have for other female filmmakers?**

HR: Fight the good fight. I think that being a woman, having children, juggling the personal and professional has made me a more interesting person with a far wider and subtler take on the world. A young single male might have more energy but he is bound to have less wisdom.

Nancy Schwartzman

DOCUMENTARY TITLE: *The Line*

Date of Release (or festival premiere): June 2009

Link to IMDb Page: http://www.imdb.com/title/tt1515933

Link to Site: http://whereisyourline.org/about/#film

Link to Trailer: http://whereisyourline.org/about

BIO: Recently named one of the "10 Filmmakers to Watch in 2011" by *Independent Magazine*, Nancy Schwartzman's work explores the intersection of sexuality, new media, and navigating partner communication about consent. She is the director and producer of the documentary film *The Line* and *xoxosms*.

Schwartzman's first documentary film, *The Line*, is a fearless twenty-four-minute documentary that chronicles one woman's personal journey after she is raped—exploring the line of consent, justice, accountability, and today's media saturated "rape culture." Launched in tandem with the film, The Line Campaign is an interactive space for dialogue about boundaries and consent.

Schwartzman's newest documentary film, *xoxosms*, follows the lives and modern love of two young adults, and explores the digital intimacy that comes with social networking technology. The film highlights the Internet as a bridge for lost souls, a lifeline for long distance relationships, and a place where love happens.

Using media and workshop discussions, Schwartzman challenges thousands of students to "think twice" and to challenge normative behavior among college youth. Schwartzman opens up a dialogue about desire, consent, and boundaries, advising student groups, faculty, and administration on how to foster healthier communities. (Credit: *The Line* Official Website)

DESCRIPTION: A one night stand far from home goes terribly wrong. As the filmmaker unravels her experience, she decides to confront her attacker.

Told through a "sex-positive" lens, *The Line* is a twenty-four-minute documentary about a young woman—the filmmaker—who is raped, but her story isn't cut and dry. Not a "perfect victim," the filmmaker confronts her attacker, recording the conversation with a hidden camera. Sex workers, survivors, and activists discuss justice, accountability, and today's "rape culture." The film asks the question: Where is the line defining consent? Shown in film festivals around the world, *The Line* was released in September 2009, and is a top-selling film with educational distributor, the Media Education Foundation. (Credit: *The Line* Official Website)

Interview Date: April 14, 2010

WOMEN AND HOLLYWOOD: **It takes a lot of guts to make a film about a difficult personal experience. Why did you feel compelled to make this film?**

NANCY SCHWARTZMAN: I was sexually assaulted while living in Jerusalem by a man I worked with and willingly went to bed with. The night took a turn for the worse, and he raped me. I was shocked and horrified. I thought no one in Jerusalem would understand that even if I were already in his bed, that this was rape.

I waited until I got back to "civilization" (i.e., New York) where I felt safer talking about what happened, to admit what happened and describe the experience. But at home, my friends, people I trusted and who cared about me, minimized the experience, found ways to blame my behavior for what happened—flirting, drinking, being an American. They told me what happened wasn't that bad.

If people had understood the definition of assault and had the courage to recognize that even when it is complicated, it still is a violation. If they had been supportive I wouldn't have needed to make this film. I wouldn't have understood how deeply we as a culture excuse and apologize for rape, assault, and violation. It gave the film a life beyond my own story, and it gave me a place to explore the complexity of the issue, both personally and politically.

W&H: **Is "the line" different for everyone? Is there more difference between men and women?**

NS: Absolutely. That diversity of expression, opinion, and prefer-
ence is what inspired the entire campaign. I wanted to capture
the conversations people were having after seeing the film, how
they thought about their own lives, what they brought back
into their bedrooms, so we asked—"Where is your line?" And
we collect the answers on our site.

W&H: **You have taken the film on the road and talked about sexual
assault. What has been the most gratifying about your travels
and what has been the most difficult?**

NS: The most gratifying is when young men who leap up in the
their seats after a screening to come and tell me how inspiring
the film is and how they feel trapped by traditional ideas of
"masculinity." They want to see a change on their campus and
in their lives. The ones who ask loudly in front of their peers
why more men don't exhibit basic emotional intelligence, and
why we let those who behave badly off the hook, and how men
cannot afford to see bad behavior and look the other way. I love
those moments.

The most difficult is the endemic nature of sexual assault.
Especially highlighting a story like mine, a rape between
friends, acquaintances, partners, or classmates. My story is so
common. I'm glad the film enables women to speak up and
share, but the numbers can be overwhelming. Ultimately, the
more we break the isolation and come together, the louder,
stronger, and angrier we get, the more chance we have to put an
end to sexual violence as a cultural norm.

W&H: **You show that a film has the ability to impact and open up a
dialogue about an important issue. Is film able to do this differently than other media?**

NS: I think storytelling—intimate, raw, honest exchanges—
whether it is spoken word, radio, performance, or film, allow

us to open up, feel, and transform. Film is so tangible, and when shared in a crowded room, in the dark, it can be a collective experience.

W&H: **Are you a filmmaker or activist first?**

NS: First and foremost, I'm a storyteller, and I want to build a community and create change around the films that I make.

W&H: **What did you learn about yourself in this process?**

NS: I crave collaboration. I hate working alone.

W&H: **What advice do you have for other filmmakers?**

NS: Partnerships are everything. Good partners and collaborators are truly a gift—they are hard to find, they are worth waiting for, and they should be treasured. Also, know your audience— especially documentary filmmakers. Let the web be your guide if you're exploring a topic. Ask, "What are they already talking about? How can you add and enhance or challenge the conversation? Make sure you love your subject matter, because you're going to be stuck with it for a long time.

ACKNOWLEDGEMENTS

There are many people to thank for supporting my work and the work of Women and Hollywood.

First, the women who are credited as co-editors on this book. They all worked many hours for free and kept me focused and moving forward. I am forever grateful to Eva Krainitzki, Laura Shields, Emilie Spiegel, Elizabeth Harper, and Heather McLendon for their help.

My family at the Athena Center for Leadership Studies at Barnard College who have helped take the work of Women and Hollywood to another level. I'm so grateful that Kitty Kolbert was inspired at an event I organized for director Jane Campion at Gloria Steinem's home and then conspired with me to come up with the Athena Film Festival. She saw potential in me that I didn't know was there. We are both lucky to have the great support of Barnard President Debora Spar.

Maria Perez Martinez is a true collaborator and I am so proud to work with her.

The interns for the Athena Film Festival—what can I say about these young women? They are so smart, so on the ball, and they do the work of people with double their experience and age. I know I will be working for them one day. They are Patricia Urena, Laura Shields, Ashley Bush, Mica Spika, Zoe LePage, Julia Kennedy, and Charlie Gillette.

The rest of the team Athena: Michael Comstock, Stephanie Berger, Stewart Berger, Hailee Greene, Matt Everett, Sara Leger, Rudy Scala, Lina Plath, Veronica Bufalini, and Clare Anne Darragh, Sun Min, Matthew Willse.

There are people who believed in me long before I believed in myself. I would never be where I am today had I not lucked into a job working for Marie C. Wilson at the Ms. Foundation for Women.

There would be no Women and Hollywood without Nancy Schwartz Sternoff and Barbara Dobkin. They supported my work from the earliest days and their belief and support kept me going.

Robin Morgan and the Sisterhood Is Global Institute for being my fiscal sponsor. And to Mary Thom for helping me to appreciate the gift of having a good editor.

Anne Thompson for recommending me to Indiewire and all the editors at Indiewire, particularly Dana Harris, for letting me write what I write.

To my friends, especially Andrea Miller and Howard May, who listen to all my stories most times not knowing who or what I am talking about, but always being the most supportive friends I could ever have. To my gym buddy Theresa Rebeck who has been a touchstone on all the issues we both care about.

To my parents—Jack and Linda—who always told my sisters, Susie and Hilary, and me that we could be or do anything we wanted to.

To the photographers and picture rights holders who allowed their photos to be published here gratis.

To all the directors who teach me so much.

Most especially to all the people who read the blog. It is because you read the site and send me your comments, ideas, and outrage that I do what I do.

I called this book **In Her Voice** because I want to hear more women's voices. Because I believe women's voices are as valuable and because students and movie lovers should be able to walk into a bookstore or type into Google and find a book on women directors. It is imperative that male and female students who are getting into the business learn about women directors just like they learn about male directors. This book is also for movie lovers who care about seeing more women onscreen and behind the scenes.

Lastly, one of the common themes you will read in interview after interview is the call to keep fighting for your vision. This is a message to women directors, producers, writers—anyone who wants to work in the business. Your voice counts. Your vision matters.

—October 2012

CPSIA information can be obtained
at www.ICGtesting.com
Printed in the USA
LVHW011340070722
722906LV00003B/216